# TENACIOUS D
## IN
# THE PICK OF DESTINY

**TENACIOUS D**
**IN**
**THE PICK OF DESTINY**
ISBN 1 84576 301 7
ISBN-13 9781845763015

Published by
Titan Books
A division of
Titan Publishing Group Ltd
144 Southwark St
London
SE1 0UP

First edition November 2006
2 4 6 8 10 9 7 5 3 1

**Special thanks to Essi Berelian, for his mammoth interview with Tenacious D,
which is featured throughout this book.**

The publishers would also like to thank Lourdes Arocho, Ed Bolkus, Amy Rivera,
Stacy Osugi and everyone at New Line; Michele Fleischli; Liam Lynch; and of
course The D themselves: Jack Black and Kyle Gass, without whom...

Book design by Martin Stiff.

Visit our website:
**www.titanbooks.com**

Did you enjoy this book? We love to hear from our readers. Please e-mail us at:
**readerfeedback@titanemail.com** or write to Reader Feedback at the above address.

To subscribe to our regular newsletter for up-to-the-minute news, great offers
and competitions, email: **titan-news@titanemail.com**

A CIP catalogue record for this title is available from the British Library.

Printed and bound in the USA.

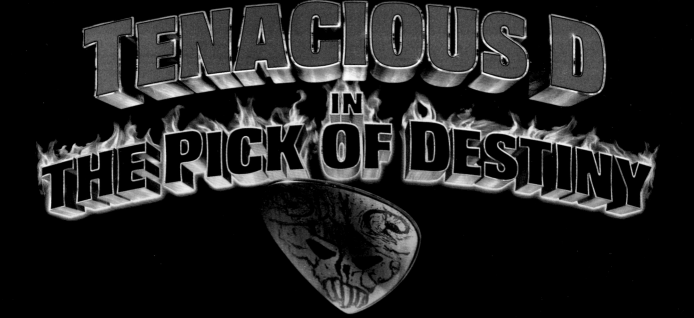

# TENACIOUS D IN THE PICK OF DESTINY

## THE GREATEST MOVIE TIE-IN BOOK IN THE WORLD

FEATURING EXTRACTS FROM THE MOTION PICTURE SCREENPLAY WRITTEN BY

## JACK BLACK & KYLE GASS & LIAM LYNCH

TITAN BOOKS

*Tribute

BE THEY ANGELS?

NAY, THEY ARE BUT MEN...

# INTRODUCING

# TENACIOUS D

JACK BLACK
AKA JB / JABLES / WONDERBOY

KYLE GASS
AKA KG / KAGE / NASTYMAN

**So guys, just in case there is anyone who has been living under a rock for the last decade, tell us: what is Tenacious D?**

**Jack:** The D are two dudes who formed a band. A band that defies description. Some have said the greatest band of all time.

**Is it possible to encapsulate the D in one word? Or in one sentence?**

**Kyle:** My one word would be: Rrrrroooockin'!

**Jack:** And my one word... interdimensional! And don't forget: 'Or in one sentence'. I'd like to give my one sentence. 'Those guys are interdimensional.'

**Kyle:** [crazy laughter] I don't even know what interdimensional means!

**Jack:** Interdimensional? It means we, like, cross dimensions.

**Kyle:** Well, I think Tenacious D is a high-octane thrill ride!

**A thrill ride to where?**

**Kyle:** [mysteriously/dramatically] To the centre of your mind.

**What is the underlying ethos of the D?**

**Jack:** The D have no ethos. We float on the breeze like an apple blossom in spring. This universe we inhabit is a large and unforgiving glory pit!

**That's extremely Zen...**

**Jack:** Wait, wait... one other thing...What is an ethos?

**Kyle:** Ethos would be a philosophy.

**Jack:** That's part of my answer though, what is an ethos? I answer the question with a question...

**Kyle:** Man, that's *deep*.

**Tenacious D in the Pick of Destiny is evidently a docudrama — a *rockudrama*, if you will — which recounts real events. How would you sum up the movie?**

**Jack:** It's the true-to-life story of how we first met and formed the band known as Tenacious D. It is also the tale of our quest to become the greatest band of all time.

**Kyle:** I would say the movie is part auto-biographical. I think it's part adventure and I think it's also part inspirational. If people wanna rock and they're not sure how, then I think if they watch the film they'll probably be inspired to rock themselves.

**Why tell this story now? Is the world ready for it?**

**Jack:** Is the world ready for it? That's like asking if a drowning man is ready for a life preserver! The world *needs* this film.

**Kyle:** It's absolutely necessary in these troubled times.

**Jack:** It may bring world peace, as well as a renaissance of super-sauce creativity! There many be dancing and singing in the street! But why tell the story now? The time was right. As Kyle and I said for years, 'We will serve no D-wine, until it's D-time.'

**Kyle:** And you know what? It is now D-time.

**Jack:** The time has come for the tale to be told, just like Gallo and their wine... When the grapes in Gallo's vineyard are ready for squeezing, Gallo *knows*. So knoweth The D, so knoweth The D.

**Was it strange to revisit this pivotal part of your lives?**

**Kyle:** I thought it was. It was surreal and disconcerting in a way. To remember a time when Jack was subservient to me, when I held the cards, when I controlled the reins. And it was actually quite satisfying, the week that we were in my apartment and Jack was doing what I told him, and he looked at me with his big saucer eyes with nothing but admiration. Then it all turned. Then it was just like today.

**Jack:** It is sometimes painful to remember our early days. It was not all wine and roses.

**Kyle:** There were some tough times.

**Jack:** It takes a lot of digging to find the diamonds of invention. And like all great collaborations there was a power struggle between us. We had to face a lot of inner demons. And some outer ones too.

**Speaking of which, how did Satan get involved as executive producer of *Tenacious D in The Pick of Destiny*?**

**Jack:** Satan has a cameo in the movie. We actually could've gotten James Earl Jones to play the role. But we really wanted Satan to play it himself, so we talked to his agent and he agreed to appear under the condition that we make him an executive producer. Unfortunately that entitles him to 66.6% of the profits of the movie.

**Kyle:** And a say in the final cut.

**Jack:** Yeah, he had the final cut 'cos he's one greedy sonofagod!

**Kyle:** The cut sort of favours his particular scenes. He'll know why.

**Jack:** But dude, don't you think we coulda got James Earl Jones to play the devil?

**Kyle:** Yeah... he's got that voice.

**Jack:** He was the voice of Darth Vader! And he was also the Snake Monster King in *Conan*.

**Kyle:** Yeah, yeah, it woulda been perfect casting. We had the real thing though I guess...

**Tell us about Liam Lynch, your director and partner in crime.**

**Kyle:** Ah, Liam. Double L.

**Jack:** Liam is a travelling vagabond visionary! He wasn't so much a director as he was a magical, mystical shaman. He would stare into the empty reaches of the universal superfreak and find us golden nuggets to juggle. He's kind of like the Silver Surfer of rock. He's also skinny and crazy creative, and smokes a pack of Carltons a day, which equals one cigarette a month!

**Kyle:** He was so positive that I was pretty sure during the making of the movie that I was going to win an Oscar.

**Jack:** [incredulous laughter]

**Kyle:** I never had a bad take, apparently. Very positive energy.

LIAM LYNCH
DIRECTOR / CO-WRITER /
MYSTICAL SHAMAN

## Kickapoo

**TENACIOUS D**
A long ass fucking time ago in a
town called Kickapoo
There lived a humble family religious thru
and thru.
But yay, there was a black sheep and he
knew just what to do.
His name was young JB and he refused
to step in line.
A vision he could see of fucking rocking
all the time.
He wrote a tasty jam and all the planets
did align.

**LIL' JB**
The dragon's balls were blazing as I
stepped into his cave,
then I sliced his fucking cockles with my
long and shiny blade!
Twas I who fucked the dragon, fuck-a-lie,
sing fuck-a-loo.
And if you try to fuck with me, then I
shall fuck you too!

**Tell us about the opening scenes of the movie, and the song 'Kickapoo'.**

**Jack:** It's a song about my tough child-hood growing up on the mean streets of Kickapoo. We got Meat Loaf to play young JB's meanass controlling dad, Bud. He blew doors down in his first movie singing performance since *The Rocky Horror Picture Show*. Then lil' JB turns to his rock poster of Ronnie James Dio for support and inspiration. To his surprise Dio comes alive and sings a blistering section of rock to shake the pillars of hell! Dio's performance is powerful, to say the least — it's mind altering. Young JB runs away from home... and thus begins *The Pick Of Destiny*.

**Kyle:** I think it's possibly the strongest opening scene in the history of motion pictures. It's almost *too* good. And the tragedy of it is, I'm not in it. Which is kind of a bummer.

**What was it like growing up in Kickapoo, JB? You were the black sheep of the family...**

**Jack:** It's not easy being an artist in a one horse town. No one understands the life of a poet.

**Was it really just a one horse town?**

**Jack:** There was only one horse in the entire town of Kickapoo, yes.

**Kyle:** Whose horse was it?

**Jack:** A guy named Larry.

**What was it like working with Meat Loaf?**

**Kyle:** We're not in that flashback scene of course, but we worked with him in the recording studio. It was like there was an aura around him. You knew there was something special going down. In fact everyone spontaneously left the studio 'cos they knew the *power* that was about to be unleashed...

**Jack:** He shook our foundations to the core. He just about blew my nuts off. He sang so good I stopped listening. It hurt to listen to it. Then he came out of the booth, threw me on the table, pulled out his fifteen-inch Bowie knife and said, 'Don't you *ever* disrespect me, son!' Then he got on his Harley and he blew outta town.

**How would you describe his place in the pantheon of rock?**

**Jack:** Meat Loaf is the Sultan of rock 'n' roll theatrical bombast and tender dramatical enterprises.

**Kyle:** Amen to that.

**Did you call him Meat, or Mr Loaf?**

**Jack:** Meat.

**Kyle:** Yeah, we were on a first name basis.

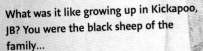

BUD BLACK
You've disobeyed my orders son, why were you ever born?
Your brother's ten times better than you. Jesus loves him more.
This music that you've played for us comes from the depths of hell.
Rock and roll's the devil's work he wants you to rebel.
You'll become a mindless puppet Beelzebub will pull the strings.
Your heart will lose direction and chaos he will bring.
You better shut your mouth, you better watch your tone.
You're grounded for a week, no telephone.
Don't let me hear you cry, don't let me hear you moan.
You gotta praise the Lord when you're in my home.

LIL' JB
Dio can you hear me?
I am lost and so alone.
I am asking for your guidance. Will you come down from your throne?
I need a tight compadre who will teach me how to rock.
My father thinks you're evil, but man he can suck a cock.
Rock is not the devil's work.
It's magical and rad.
I'll never rock as long as I am stuck here with my Dad.

**Why was your guitar called Monster Mash?**
Jack: I named it that because I love monsters and I still do. They are strong and scary. They have powers.

**Tell us about working with Ronnie James Dio.**

**Jack:** No one rocks like Dio, no one. He nailed it in one take, blistering vocal. But then he said, 'Lemme have another!' And he rocked so hard that the walls of the studio shivered and fell down around us. Then we spent six months rebuilding the studio with extra steel fortifications, but he destroyed that studio with his singing as well! So then we just ended up recording it on top of a mountain in the Himalayas.

**How about his place in the pantheon of rock?**

**Jack:** He is alone on a Rushmore unto himself.

**It's true that Dio has rocked for a long, long time: did he hand over his cape and sceptre? Did he mix his sauce with yours? Was there goulash?**

**Jack:** He did hand over a symbolic torch in an ancient torch-passing ceremony, and we did drink deep from a goulash that he made from his grandmother's famous recipe.

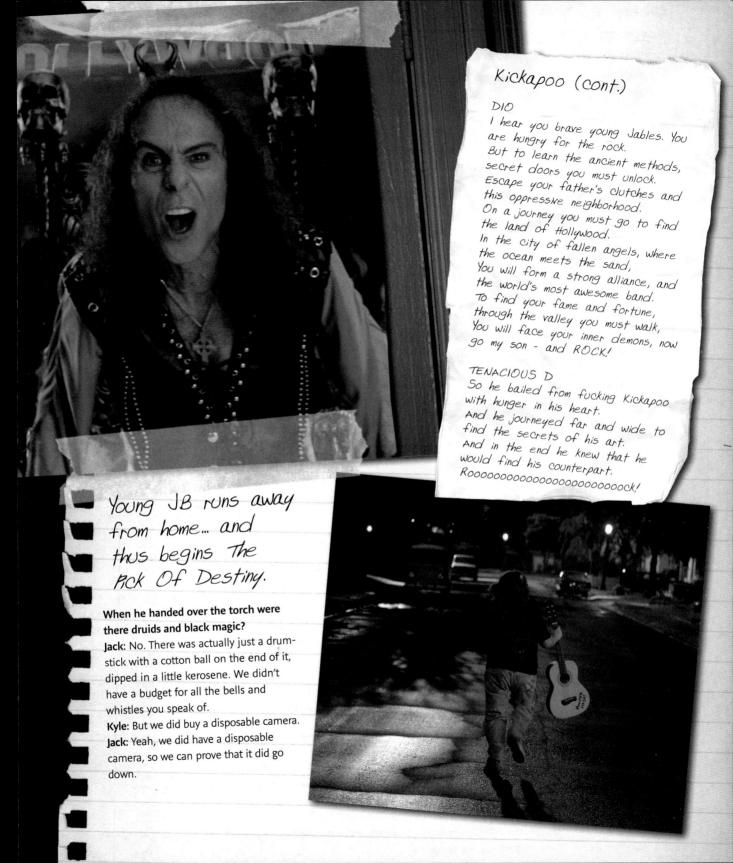

## Kickapoo (cont.)

**DIO**
I hear you brave young Jables. You
are hungry for the rock.
But to learn the ancient methods,
secret doors you must unlock.
Escape your father's clutches and
this oppressive neighborhood.
On a journey you must go to find
the land of Hollywood.
In the city of fallen angels, where
the ocean meets the sand,
You will form a strong alliance, and
the world's most awesome band.
To find your fame and fortune,
through the valley you must walk,
You will face your inner demons, now
go my son - and ROCK!

**TENACIOUS D**
So he bailed from fucking Kickapoo
with hunger in his heart.
And he journeyed far and wide to
find the secrets of his art.
And in the end he knew that he
would find his counterpart.
Rooooooooooooooooooooooooock!

Young JB runs away
from home... and
thus begins The
Pick Of Destiny.

**When he handed over the torch were
there druids and black magic?**
**Jack:** No. There was actually just a drum-
stick with a cotton ball on the end of it,
dipped in a little kerosene. We didn't
have a budget for all the bells and
whistles you speak of.
**Kyle:** But we did buy a disposable camera.
**Jack:** Yeah, we did have a disposable
camera, so we can prove that it did go
down.

It took you a while to find the actual Hollywood in California, JB. You went via Hollywood, Florida, not to mention Hollywoods in Alabama, Maryland and South Carolina. Will we ever discover what you got up to during those long years you spent, growing up on the road?

**Kyle:** I guess it's time to tell 'em. There is a prequel. Just as *Star Wars* started in the middle.

**Jack:** We're actually in negotiations to make that into a TV series, sorta like *Kung Fu.*

**Kyle:** *Jables: The Early Years?*

**Jack:** Yeah, where Jables is just wandering the land looking for Hollywood.

**Kyle:** Do you know what they should call it? *Jables' Journey.*

**Jack:** *Jables' Journey: Lookin' For Hollywood.*

**Kyle:** Yeah, a different Hollywood each week!

HOLLYWOOD

HOLLYWOOD, AL 198
PM
JUN
1981

POST CARD

EXT. VENICE BEACH – DAY

JB
Oh my god! That was the best thing I've
ever heard. Who are you?

KG
(smug)
The name's Kyle Gass.

JB
Will you teach me that thing you were
just doing? That one part...

A small crowd of tourists approach KG
and JB.

KG
I don't give free lessons. Now, why don't
you stand over there. I got a show to do.

KG starts to play for the tourists but
they simply pass by him uninterested.

JB
Man, they're stupid.

(to tourists)
Don't you guys know genius when you
see it?! Damn!

JB plays it cool.

JB (cont'd)
Anyway... my name's JB. I just rolled
into town and I was looking to start a
band. Do you want to be in a band...
with me?

KG
(not listening, looking
at tourists pass)
Hey give me some space man. Can't
you see you're cramping my style?
You're driving away my crowd...
Didn't I just tell you to go stand over
there?

A crowd approaches and KG pushes JB aside to play for the passing group. They stop for a moment to listen. JB stands a few feet to the side of KG.

JB tries to join in on KG's melody and sings over his playing. KG shoots him with vicious looks to make him stop singing, but JB feels that they are jamming together. Though KG is angry, the crowd seems to like it.

JB
(singing improvised lyrics)
Can't you see he is rad? Let me hear you applaud.
He is more than a man, he's a shiny golden god...

KG is annoyed but more people begin to gather. One tall geeky guy in a Pizza Delivery hat (Lee) is amazed by the duo.

The song ends and there is a smattering of applause. A few people throw some change into KG's open guitar case. A few walk away but Lee stays behind.

LEE
Man, that was awesome! You guys were like electric dynamite! What's the name of your band?

KG is repulsed at the thought.

KG
(to Lee – pompous)
We aren't a "band".

(to JB – cold)
They call me KG, solo-man 5000 and I aims to keep it that way! I'm out of here! This place is tapped.

He throws his guitar pick at JB to emphasize his point.

KG grabs his things and storms off.

LEE
Geez...

JB's eyes are glued to KG walking into the distance.

JB
(watching KG)
No, it's okay. It's part of his genius.

Lee Lee Lee Lee Lee Lee Lee Lee Lee,
We're talkin' fuckin' Lee.

I'm just a babbyyyyyyyyyyyyy!!!

**The fateful day you met at Venice Beach — KG was not too keen to team up at first. Why? You saw yourself as a solo artist?**

**Kyle:** Yeah, I really didn't think I needed anyone. And he seemed a little annoying, I gotta say. He started jamming with me. It was a little bit irritating. But then, I dunno, he stopped being Jables and started looking like a dollar sign. And so I brought him home.

**Jack:** I think Kage felt threatened by my sauce.

**Kyle:** All right! It's true! I did feel threatened!

**But Lee saw your potential as a duo straight away. Tell us about Lee... were you scared of him at first?**

**Kyle:** It's weird. He's so...it's almost like he's so innocuous I never really even noticed him. He seemed to be there at crucial times and yet he didn't really seem to have any impact. But I guess he really did recognise the power of the duo.

**Jack:** Lee's enthusiasm was infectious from the get go. Everyone needs a psycho fan sometimes. It gives a little rocket boost to the old ego, but yeah, his shit can be scary!

**JB is left alone with nowhere to go that night, and rocks himself to sleep. Tell us about that song. It has a plaintive quality...**

**Jack:** We just wanted to write a beautiful lullaby.

**Kyle:** A tender lullaby. It was a sweet nugget that just came outta nowhere.

EXT. BOARDWALK – NIGHT

           GANG LEADER
What have we here my little snoggles?!

           GANG MEMBER 2
I spy a stinkin' filthy fatty singing a
stupid little ditty.

           GANG MEMBER 3
And squeelin' boo hoo hoo like a weeee
baby.

           GANG MEMBER 4
Huh huh huh... weeee baby.

They rummage through his backpack,
only finding notebooks filled with
lyrics.

           GANG MEMBER 2
           (reading from notebook)
"Climb upon my faithful steed"?... This
little piggy fancies himself a poet!

He throws the notebooks to the ground.

One gang member holds his guitar and
looks it over.

           GANG MEMBER 3
What's this wonky piece of shite?
Dost thou thinkest thineself a
troubadour?!

           GANG LEADER
I think this squatty zit needs a popping
my brothers.

           GANG MEMBER 4
Huh huh huh squatty.

CUT TO:

EXT. NEARBY ON THE BOARDWALK

KG is walking home with his guitar case. He sees the gang members and JB up ahead. He hides behind some trash cans at the sign of trouble. He stays out of sight but watches the scene play out.

He hears JB yell.

                    JB (O.C.)
HEY! No, give me that! That's my lucky guitar pick!

EXT. GANG MEMBER SCENE

CUT TO:

JB pulls the pick away from one of the gang members and takes a swing at him. The gang members move in and beat the shit out of JB.

                    GANG LEADER
Time for a bit o' the old black and blue laddies!

They surround JB and all begin hitting him.

It is painful for KG to watch. He stays hidden and looks scared and concerned. The gang members leave JB unconscious in the middle of the boardwalk. One of them tosses his guitar at him and it hits him in the head. He lays there battered and bruised. Once the gang members are at a safe distance, KG comes out from

his hiding spot and walks over to JB's body on the ground.

In the center of JB's limp hand is the pick that reads "KG". JB begins to wake up so KG yells into the distance as if he was the one that scared off the attackers.

                    KG
(to gang in the distance)
That's right. Run! Unless you want some more of this!

KG does some fake karate moves.

A groggy JB smiles and looks at KG as if he were an angel standing over him.

                    JB
KG... You saved me.

                    KG
It was nothing man. They had it comin'.

                    JB
Thanks man. How can I repay you?

                    KG
...We'll figure something out.

*Climb upon my faithful steed*
*Then we gonna ride, gonna smoke some weed*

**The TRAINING.**

"Your training starts tomorrow
at the crack of noon…"

INT. KG'S APARTMENT

JB
Wow! Cool pad. You got this whole place to yourself?

KG
Yeah, I like to keep it simple. This is where I stay when I'm writing. It's minimal. Nothing to get in the way of the creative juices.

JB
Cool!

KG
Yeah, I'm working on my new album now...

He points to a cheap tape recorder sitting on a crate.

KG (cont'd)
The Kyle Gass Project. There's going to be some pretty breakthrough shit on it. I'm trying to keep it on the hush-hush though.

JB
I totally understand! I won't tell anybody! Man, if you need a singer... I am so there. Check it out...
          (sings a piece of a Dio song)
That's a Ronnie James Dio song...

KG
I know. I helped write that. I jam with him all the time.

JB
No way... You know Dio?!

KG
Sure. Dio... I know all the dudes – In Sabbath.

JB
Dude. Do you think there's any way I could maybe audition to be in the Kyle Gass Project?

KG
Maybe. In time. You got to get your chops up before you shred with big dogs, son. You got a lot to learn.

JB
Will you teach me your ways?

KG sighs and stands.

KG
I will teach you. Sleep on the power couch. Your training begins tomorrow at the crack of noon...

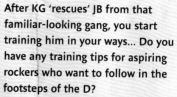

**After KG 'rescues' JB from that familiar-looking gang, you start training him in your ways... Do you have any training tips for aspiring rockers who want to follow in the footsteps of the D?**

**Kyle:** Yeah, I think try to eat right and get enough sleep. Practicing is really overrated. I don't think it's important to practice that much. Wait for lightning to strike in a bottle. And find a tremendous partner, like Jack, to work with.

**Jack:** I can't believe that one of the things you should do is to wait for lightning to strike in a bottle!

**Kyle:** Yeah. That's why, if you've noticed, the players who've practiced the most usually aren't the ones you wanna listen to. It's more about the lightning, I think.

**Jack:** The other day I met this composer who was, like, a very successful film composer. Dude didn't really know how to play piano. He never learned. And he says 'Not important'. In fact it would hurt his writing.

**Kyle:** You know, I'm kinda there now...

**Jack:** I have a training tip. Learn from the masters. Learn their songs and their ways. Study why they are so kickass. Only then can you carry on their kickassessessness. In other words: buy our first album.

**Kyle:** Love that kickassessessness!

**Jack:** Kickassessessness! There's an extra 'essess'!!

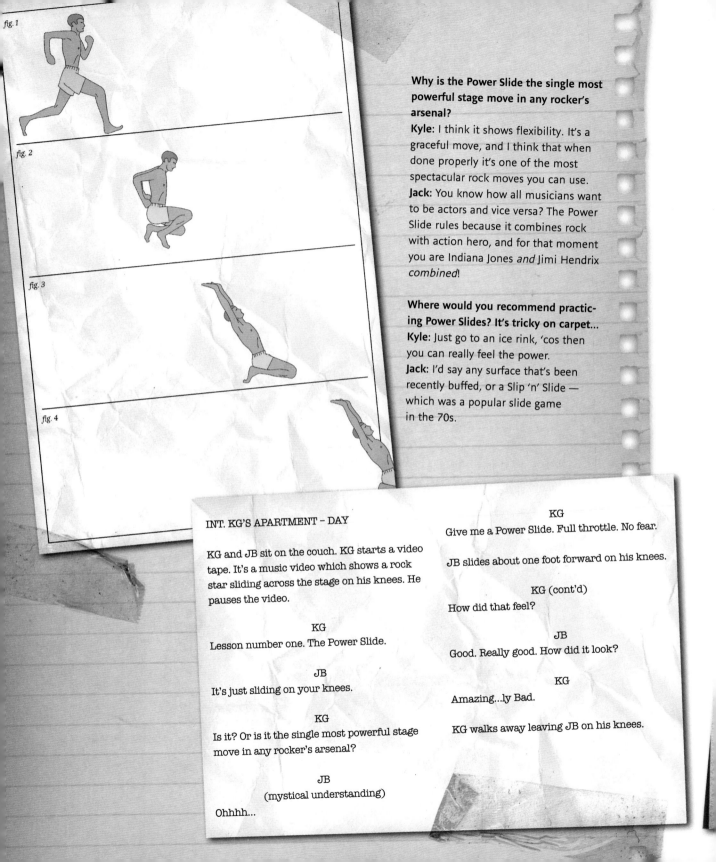

fig. 1

fig. 2

fig. 3

fig. 4

**Why is the Power Slide the single most powerful stage move in any rocker's arsenal?**

**Kyle:** I think it shows flexibility. It's a graceful move, and I think that when done properly it's one of the most spectacular rock moves you can use.

**Jack:** You know how all musicians want to be actors and vice versa? The Power Slide rules because it combines rock with action hero, and for that moment you are Indiana Jones *and* Jimi Hendrix *combined*!

**Where would you recommend practicing Power Slides? It's tricky on carpet...**

**Kyle:** Just go to an ice rink, 'cos then you can really feel the power.

**Jack:** I'd say any surface that's been recently buffed, or a Slip 'n' Slide — which was a popular slide game in the 70s.

---

INT. KG'S APARTMENT – DAY

KG and JB sit on the couch. KG starts a video tape. It's a music video which shows a rock star sliding across the stage on his knees. He pauses the video.

                    KG
Lesson number one. The Power Slide.

                    JB
It's just sliding on your knees.

                    KG
Is it? Or is it the single most powerful stage move in any rocker's arsenal?

                    JB
              (mystical understanding)
Ohhhh...

                    KG
Give me a Power Slide. Full throttle. No fear.

JB slides about one foot forward on his knees.

                    KG (cont'd)
How did that feel?

                    JB
Good. Really good. How did it look?

                    KG
Amazing...ly Bad.

KG walks away leaving JB on his knees.

INT. KG'S APARTMENT – ANOTHER DAY

KG lays on the couch watching TV and eating Honeycomb cereal. JB is massaging KG's feet.

KG

Deeper.

JB

Is this another rock lesson?

KG

This is the perfect exercise to work the baby fat off your weak ass fingers.

JB

Yeah, fuck. I'm really feeling the burn.

KG raises his empty cereal bowl.

JB

You need me to get you some more cereal?

KG

No. Take the bowl and clean it and while you're at it, clean the whole apartment.

JB

Will that help me get in the Kyle Gass Project?

KG

It couldn't hurt...

JB starts to clean the kitchen. He finds a check for two hundred dollars under the refrigerator. He jumps up.

JB

Hey, what's this check for 200 bucks?

KG is instantly in frame and yanks it from his hand.

KG
(bluffing on the spot)

Give me that. That's just a... royalty check.

JB

Why does it say, "I love you, Pumpkin" on it?

KG

That was the name of the song... It was a big hit in Canada. Get back to work!

JB
(blown away)

Cooooool.

**Rock historians need to know KG: did the Kyle Gass Project ever record any songs? You were aiming for some "pretty breakthrough shit"...**
Kyle: Yeah, well I was lying. I think that I had made some demos but that's as far as it went.

**If you had ever finished it, what would the Kyle Gass Project album have been called?**
Kyle: Hmmm...
Jack: I have one possibility: Snausages.
Kyle: How about Nuggets Of Splendor?
Jack: Nice!

**If you'd never met, and both became solo artists, what would Jack have called himself?**
Jack: I'd have to go with either Blackhole, or Tender Vittles.
Kyle: What about the Jack Black Experience?
Jack: I like it! Yes, the Jack Black Experience.

THE KYLE GASS PROJECT

NUGGETS OF SPLENDOR

INT. KG'S APPARTMENT

**KG**

Sex is a crucial component to the Kyle Gass Project. Now drop and give me one cock push-up.

**JB**

What's a cock push-up?

**KG**

It's where you lay on your stomach and you lift yourself off the ground with nothing but your boner... The cock's a muscle... you have to learn how to flex it. From now on you will do one cock push-up a day. Every day... We got to get you in shape. You never know when you'll need to fuck your way out of a tight situation.

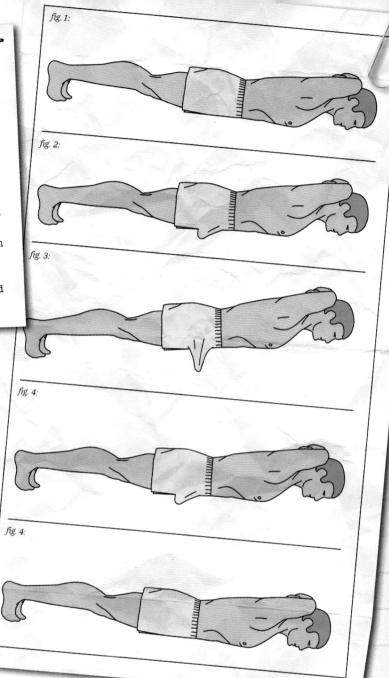

fig. 1:

fig. 2:

fig. 3:

fig. 4:

fig. 4:

**What is the best way to practice cock push-ups?**

Kyle: There's only one way really. You know Sammy Hagar says, 'There's only one way to rock'? Well, there's only one way to cock push-up.

Jack: Let me just say this: do not try to bone up and then just lay on top of it. You can break a cock. I learned that — the hard way.

**Any recommended reading material to help you get in the right frame of mind?**

Kyle: I don't think reading's important really. Except for this book.

Jack: He means for getting hard.

Kyle: Oh, for doing a cock push-up?

Jack: Yeah, to get you in the right frame of mind for a cock push-up — well you know, it's different strokes for different folks' cocks. Me personally, I like to read something that shows vaginas in it.

Kyle: [trouser-ripping laughter]

Jack: ...but that's not for everyone.

Kyle: I'd go for the story of caves. I like to go for more of a metaphor.

Jack: [mishearing] What? The Story of Kage? You would read your own auto-biography to get hard?

Kyle: No. *Caves.* Guys going spelunking.

I think that's what I would read.

Jack: [uncontrollable laughter]

Kyle: ...and that would get me really hot.

And when I've learned all of his lessons then I'll know the ancient secrets of his rock!

EXT. BOARDWALK – DAY

JB
I did it man. I made ten bucks. The training is working! I made ten whole bucks with my rock!

KG
Good. Now go score me a dime bag.

JB
A what?

KG
A dime bag. Ten dollars' worth of weed. Now listen, go down to Wake & Bake Pizzeria, ask for Jo Jo and tell him you want "The Bob Marley, extra crispy". He'll know what you're talking about.

JB
Roger that.

INT. KG'S APARTMENT

KG

It's time for your next test. Maximum Over Thruster.

JB

A video game?

KG

So much more than a game... It's a virtual meditation. I want you to play it no less than five hours a day.

JB

Five hours?

KG

Yes. It sharpens the senses and keeps the mind frosty. It helps one to achieve perfect inner calm. I'm on the final level.

**KG, tell us about the meditative powers of Maximum Over Thruster
Kyle:** Well, it really uses all of your faculties, your eyesight, your reflexes, your hearing. And to perform at a really high level you have to be completely focused. So I think it's just great training for music and life, and if you also wanna be a racing car driver like Andrew Ridgeley.

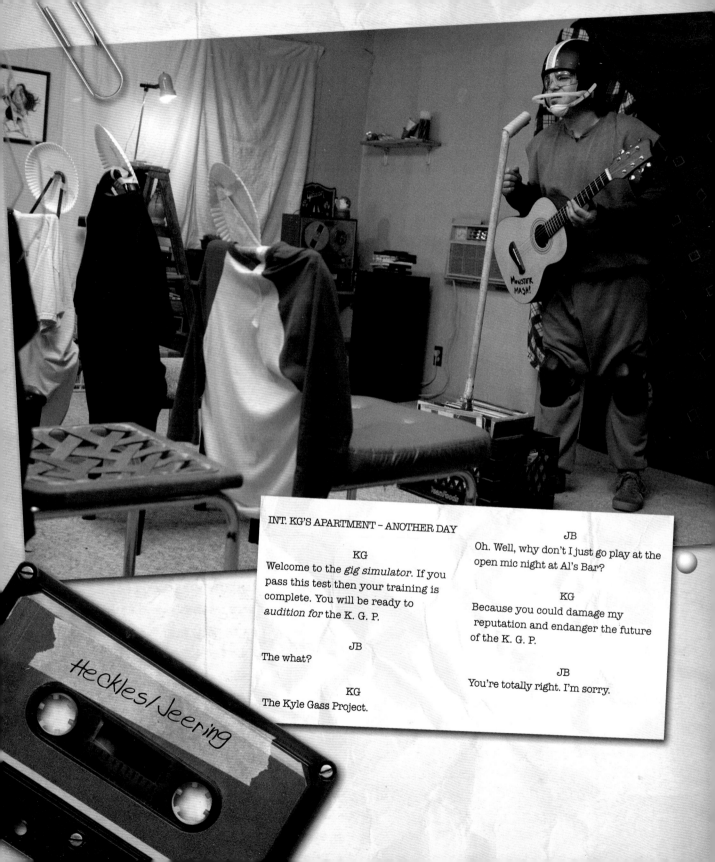

INT. KG'S APARTMENT – ANOTHER DAY

KG
Welcome to the *gig simulator*. If you pass this test then your training is complete. You will be ready to *audition for* the K. G. P.

JB
The what?

KG
The Kyle Gass Project.

JB
Oh. Well, why don't I just go play at the open mic night at Al's Bar?

KG
Because you could damage my reputation and endanger the future of the K. G. P.

JB
You're totally right. I'm sorry.

Heckles/Jeering

**Tell us about the gig simulator. Why was it created? You had a tough experience, JB.**

**Jack:** Well, it's a training tool like the army would use for dangerous scenarios, so must we prepare for the sometimes deadly world of rock. I fumbled my first time out. It's to be expected.

**Kyle:** It's really to replicate the pressure, the *danger* of a live performance, without actually having to be at the gig. It has the added dangers I programmed in, like the flying bottles and such, but you're still in the safety of your own home.

**Jack:** I was thinking, Kage, you know what would be a really good simulator? A bull fighting simulator.

**Kyle:** A bullfighting simulator would be awesome.

**Jack:** Wouldn't that be a fucking great simulator?

**Kyle:** Otherwise, you know, how do you practice bullfighting?

**Jack:** *Exactly.*

**Kyle:** Do you go in with a small bull at first? You'd start with a cow maybe...

So must we prepare for the sometimes deadly world of rock.

INT. KG'S APARTMENT

JB

Um... Should I play a song?

Kyle presses the play button on his tape recorder.

TAPE RECORDED VOICE
Come on, play a song ass face!

CUT TO:

The voice is clearly KG trying to sound like someone else.

JB

Oh... Okay. Um, I'm JB from the Kyle Gass Project...

The tape recorder sounds again.

TAPE RECORDED VOICE
Get on with it dumb shit!

JB

Oh, okay...

JB starts to play and sing a song about KG and the Kyle Gass Project.

JB (cont'd)
(singing)
The Kyle Gass Project is out of control...

The tape recorder sounds again.

TAPE RECORDED VOICE
Get off the stage! You stupid dilweed!

JB
(singing)
He turned me to a diamond from a piece of coal!

KG presses play on the recorder again and he can be heard "booing".

TAPE RECORDED VOICE
Boo! Boooooo!

The booing interferes with JB's concentration and he misses a chord on his guitar.

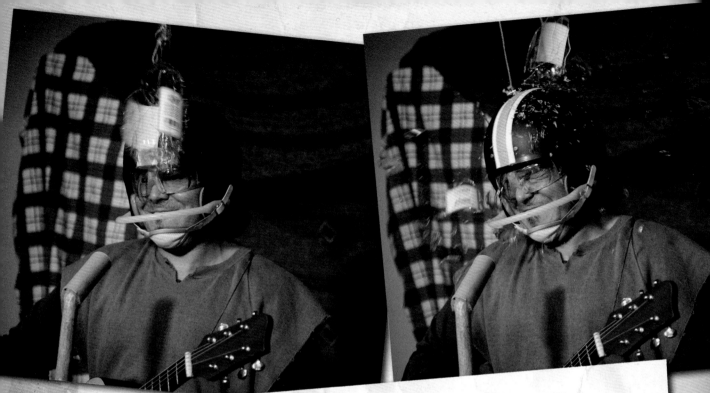

As he struggles to find the chord, KG cuts a string which sends an empty beer bottle swinging towards JB's head. The bottle smashes against his helmet.

> JB
>
> AHH!

KG presses play on the tape player again.

> TAPE RECORDED VOICE
>
> Go back to Kickapoo, you fat-ass momma's boy!

> JB
> (singing, worried, in pain)
> He teaches me the secrets of the pumpkin patch!

JB begins to tremble. He continues to try to rock.

KG cuts another string. An empty Jack Daniels bottle swings down from the ceiling and smashes against JB's helmet. JB is knocked senseless for a moment. His eyes glaze over.

JB stops playing altogether. He is fumbling with the microphone and lost.

> TAPE RECORDED VOICE
>
> Booooo! Booooo! Boo!

A thousand "boo"s.

> JB
> (to himself)
> Um... Power slide.

JB only has one trick left... the power slide. He attempts to slide but his momentum causes him to be thrown forward onto his stomach crushing Monster Mash flat.

He sits up with his guitar in splinters – He leans back onto his knees and is frozen in shock.

Still in his power slide pose, JB begins to weep like a baby. KG turns off the tape recorded booing.

> KG
>
> He's had enough. Lights!

Lee flips the switch and turns on the apartment lights.

KG comes over to the crumpled JB and touches his head.

> KG
> (consoling)
> Hey... It's okay. Don't worry.

> JB
> (crying)
> ...I suck. I suck.

> KG
>
> You don't suck. You think I'd be wasting my time if I didn't see something special in you. You just weren't ready yet. I should have known you weren't ready. Nobody passes the gig simulator the first time... not even this guy. Now let's clean this place up. What do you say?

The D are now seasoned live performers of course, but you must have had your share of hecklers over the years. What are the best heckles you've ever heard?

**Jack:** What is the point of a heckle? The point of the heckle is to take attention away from the people on stage and put it onto you, lonesome, sad audience member that wishes you were on stage. That's what the heckler does. But when you say the *best* heckle you must mean the most *painful*, the one that inflicts the most pain. Not just funny. One time when we were on stage, someone in the audience yelled out, 'You are *not* completely blowing my mind right at this moment!'

**Kyle:** [wild laughter]

**Jack:** And that hurt.

**Kyle:** [sounds like he's dying]

**Jack:** Even though right before that he screamed, 'You are completely blowing my mind!' And right after, 'You are again now blowing my mind!' Still, for that one moment when he said we weren't blowing his mind, it was one of the most painful heckles.

**What about the best heckle you ever gave?**

**Jack:** I have a favourite. When I don't like what I'm hearing or seeing, I will yell out, 'You are not good at playing music!'

**Kyle:** [sounds like he's dying again]

**Jack:** And if I really wanna sting 'em I'll get specific, like, 'With your fingers on the guitar!'

INT. KG'S APARTMENT

The phone has started ringing and on the second ring, the answering machine picks up.

                    FEMALE VOICE
                 (coming from machine)
Hi Pumpkin, it's your mother. Your father and I have decided that fifteen years of trying to be a famous musician is long enough. So I'm sorry to say we aren't going to be sending you any more rent checks. It's time to get a real job. I love you Pumpkin!

KG is frozen in fear. His secret is out.

JB realizes that KG has lied to him about the checks and probably everything else as well.

                    JB
Pumpkin?! Those weren't royalty checks...

Jack soon finds out KG's true nature, not to mention his true hairstyle. Did you feel betrayed JB?

**Jack:** Oh god, yes! I was played like a tin fiddle at a country-time jamboree!

**And what was the tune being played upon you?**

**Kyle:** I Want Your Sex by George Michael?

**Jack:** I imagine it was more like, that song from the movie with 'Squeal like a pig!' in it... More like a *Deliverance* theme.

**Kyle:** Duelling Banjos!

**Jack:** Yeah, those were my emotions being played! My heartstrings being plucked! Like this! [Tries to imitate a banjo being played by Eddie Van Halen.]

**We get a glimpse of young Kyle. Not a happy childhood?**

**Kyle:** No. Obviously having male pattern baldness at the age of eight can alienate you from the other kids. They called me Baldy. Shiny. Cueball. It was painful. They also called me Gasser. Lots of meanness.

**Jack:** It was a painful snippet from his youth.

**Kyle:** Indeed it was. It was hard for me back then, it scarred me. That's why I developed my other skills. I always felt I needed to prove myself.

**But coming back to that moment of betrayal: little did either of you know that your destiny was at hand... that a mystical convergence of signs was about to give a mighty band its name...**

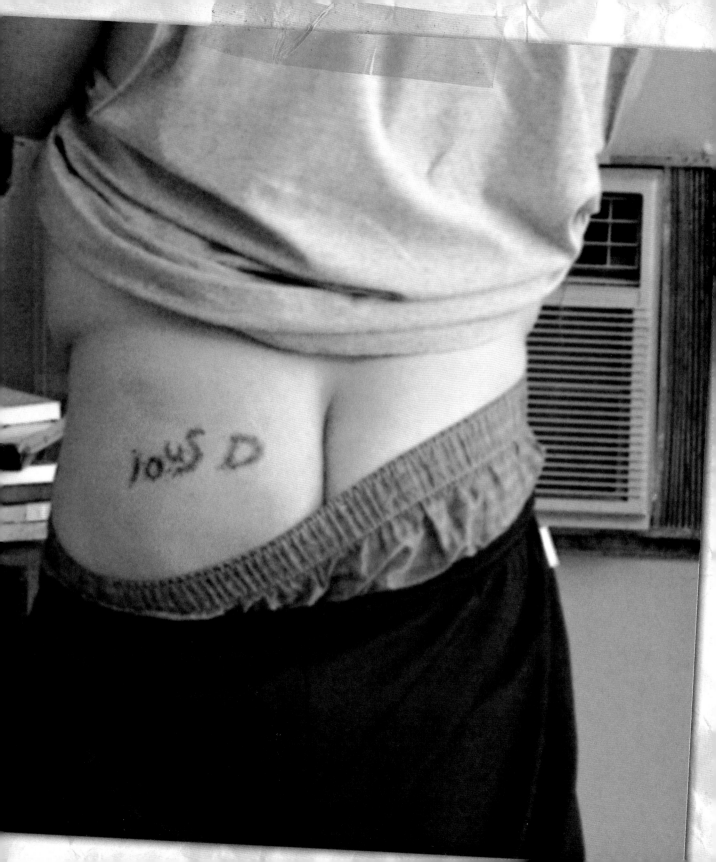

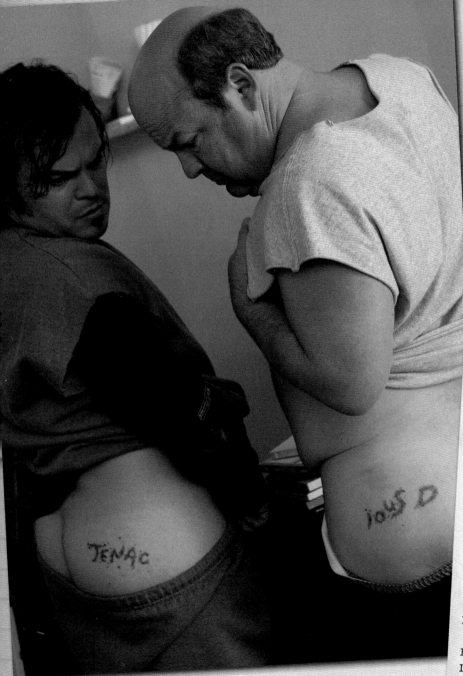

**Tell us about the moment that your
asses shaped the future of rock
history, and a band was born...**
Jack: I cried when I saw the recreation
of that momentous occasion. When
those butts came together, well,
sometimes the planets align.

Kyle: You know what? The crazy thing
is that I wasn't even fully aware of how
it all came together until I saw the
movie, 'cos I couldn't see my own butt
at the time. I just thought Jack came
up with a new name. He probably
wanted to touch my butt with his.

stares at the shiny new guitar.

KG starts packing again.

JB

Stop packing, dude. We're gonna pay the rent... with our rock!

KG

We are?

JB

Yeah, but we're not going to be called the "Kyle Gass Project"... From now on we will be known as Tenac.

KG

Tenac? What's that?

JB

It's a sign. A legacy I've carried with me my whole life.

JB turns around, shows a birthmark on his right butt cheek. The splotchy birthmark seems to spell the word "TENAC".

JB

I've had this birthmark since I was born. I looked it up and I think it means "Lost Traveler" in Eskimo. I never knew why I had it, but it's clear to me now. It's the name of our fuckin' band, dude.

KG marvels at the birthmark. He stands up slowly.

KG

I have a birthmark too...

KG turns and reveals a birthmark on his left butt cheek that seems to spell "IOUSD"

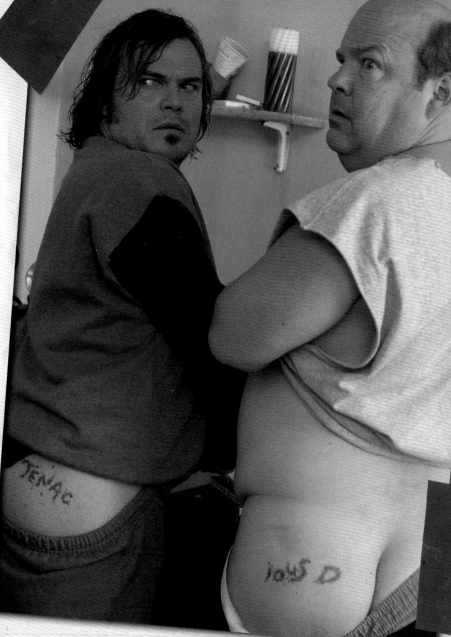

**Jack, was it a sneaky way of getting your butt next to Kyle's?**
**Jack:** Well, I don't know what you are suggesting! What's significant to me is when those two butts come together they create a third butt, because my right cheek and Kyle's left cheek are squished together to create, like, another ass. Half my ass, half Kyle's ass. When you look at our two butts, there's three cracks now, my crack, his crack and the crack we create between us!
**Kyle:** You, me and the crack we create!
**Jack:** That should have been the name of the movie!

~~IOUSD TENAC?~~ TENACIOUS D!

DESTINY.

"Since the beginning of time,
'twas written in the stones that
one day a band would come…"

INT. AL'S BAR

OPEN MIC HOST

This next act asked me to read this...
"Since the beginning of time, twas
written in the stones that one day a
band would come. Well that band has
come and now they're here to cum
again in your ear pussies. Ladies and
gentlemen, Tenacious D".

Tenacious D take the stage and
immediately launch into the song,
'History of Tenacious D'

## History of Tenacious D

We ride with kings on mighty steeds, across the devil's plain.
We've walked with Jesus and his cross,
He did not die in vain, no!
We've run with wolves. We've climbed K-2. Even stopped a moving train.
We've traveled through space and time my friend to rock this house again!
We ride and we ride and we'll never subside and we'll ride till the planets collide.
And if you say we do not ride I'll tan your fucking hide.
Ride!
Kyle's fingers be silver.
Jack's voice then be gold.
But lest you think we're vain,
We know you're all robots and we don't care.
Tenacious D,
We reign!
We reign,
Supreme, oh God!
Burrito supreme,
And a chicken supreme,
And a cutlass supreme.
Supreme, yeah. Go now Kyle, 123.
Supreme!

**Tell us about the song 'History of Tenacious D'.**

**Jack:** It is what it says it is. Both a list of things we have done in the past and a chronicling of our rise to power. What else can you say about that song other than what it is?

**Kyle:** It's not really chock full of metaphor. It's spelled out for you. It's a docu-song, our docu-tune.

The open mic host shrugs unimpressed.

OPEN MIC HOST
It was okay.

JB
It was okay? You were okay. *We were kick ass* and we're gonna totally win that money next week at the open mic contest!

OPEN MIC HOST
(unconvinced)
Good luck... there's some pretty stiff competition. Don't count your chickens. Hey, might want to work up some new material though.

JB walks out of the bar in a huff.

EXT. ALLEY WAY NEXT TO AL'S BAR

Outside, Lee and KG celebrate the performance but JB seems unsatisfied.

LEE
That was amazing! You changed people's lives tonight!

KG
I know! We were so awesome, dude!

JB is brooding.

JB
Yeah, we were awesome... compared to BULLSHIT! But compared to the GREATS? To fucking Zeppelin? Compared to the fucking Beatles? To Beethoven?

Dude, look, true we did kick ass but if we want to win that fucking money (points to contest sign on door) we're going to have to write a fucking *MASTERPIECE*. The Doors had THE

The song is met with a smattering of applause. They bound off the stage triumphantly. Lee joins them, wearing a handmade Tenacious D T-shirt. JB sees the open mic host and goes to speak to him.

JB
(to KG and Lee)
Wait for me outside. I'm going to talk to the big cheese.

JB goes to the side of the stage and speaks to the open mic host.

JB
(enthusiastic)
Well? So what'd you think?

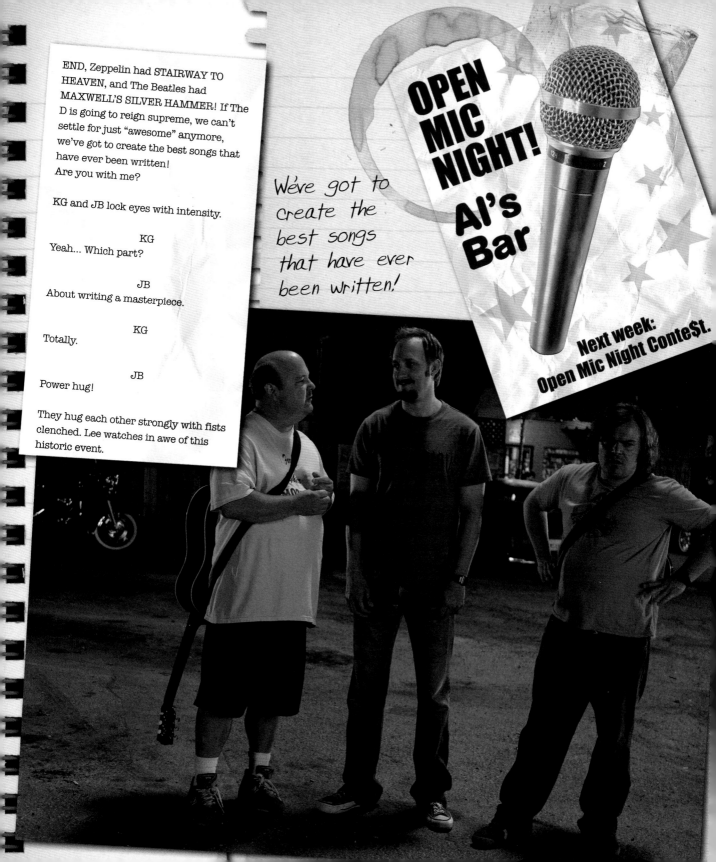

END, Zeppelin had STAIRWAY TO HEAVEN, and The Beatles had MAXWELL'S SILVER HAMMER! If The D is going to reign supreme, we can't settle for just "awesome" anymore, we've got to create the best songs that have ever been written!
Are you with me?

KG and JB lock eyes with intensity.

                    KG
Yeah... Which part?

                    JB
About writing a masterpiece.

                    KG
Totally.

                    JB
Power hug!

They hug each other strongly with fists clenched. Lee watches in awe of this historic event.

We've got to create the best songs that have ever been written!

**OPEN MIC NIGHT!**

**Al's Bar**

Next week: Open Mic Night Conte$t.

The MASTERPIECE.

"Don't make a sound unless it's a masterpiece. Not a sound."

INT. KG'S APARTMENT

JB and KG sit at the kitchen table with their guitars. The tape recorder sits on the table.

JB

Alright dude, this is it. Don't make a sound unless it's a masterpiece. Not a sound.

KG

Yeah, but how will we know if it's a masterpiece?

JB

You'll feel it and when you feel it press record and lay it on me, brother.

JB and KG sit in silence looking each other in the eyes for 15 seconds. KG's eyes widen as he slowly nods his head. JB gives him a nod to press record. KG presses record and then rips a huge fart.

KG

...I thought I felt something.

There is a pause.

JB

Let's hear that back.

MASTERPIECES

Don't Stop Believin' — Journey
Dust In The Wind — Kansas
The Grand Illusion — Styx
The End — The Doors
Stairway — Led Zep
Maxwell's Silver Hammer — The Beatles

**Where does inspiration come from? How does one go to Inspirado?**

Kyle: Very, very good question.

Jack: I like to sit quietly and close my eyes and wait for the answers to come to my brain pan.

**Cool. They just arrive, do they?**

Jack: Well, you have to look for them. I just like to sit there quietly, like a cat in front of a mouse hole. Cos I know that fuckin' juicy nugget is gonna come through that hole if I just wait with stillness and patience. And then you pounce on it.

Kyle: I usually wait for God to whisper in my ear with chord changes.

**Wow. So the Almighty is actually a co-writer on some of your tunes?**

Kyle: Well, yes. Sometimes he'll whisper, 'A minor.' And I'll go, 'What? Oh, OK...' I start playing an A minor and Jack takes it and runs.

I USUALLY WAIT FOR GOD TO WHISPER IN MY EAR WITH CHORD CHANGES.

D F#M
EM A
D F#M

INT. KG'S APARTMENT –
THE NEXT DAY

The room is set for a symbolic
ceremony. The furniture has been
pushed aside. Candles form a circle on
the floor. The tape recorder sits in its
center. JB is closing the circle by
squeezing a line of ketchup straight
onto the carpet. He tosses the bottle
aside.

                    JB
          (whispered intensity)
Okay, no more fucking around. The
masterpiece is right in there. All we
have to do is step into the magic circle
and the fucking masterpiece is ours.
Are you ready? Are you ready to write
a fucking masterpiece? Because I sure
the fuck am!

KG is game.

                    KG
Yeah!

                    JB
Let's go.

They step across the line of ketchup. JB
is instantly in a state of panic.

                    JB
What are you doing? Go! Play something! The magic only lasts a second!

KG starts playing.

                    JB
That's horrible! Where's the passion?
Feel it! Grab it! Taste it! What the fuck
was that? You're losing it for us! Play

Something! Better! Faster! Juicier!
Wait! Keep playing that! That's it!

JB begins to improv sing to the guitar
riff but stops short.

                    JB
Are we recording? Press RECORD!
Press Record! Too late. We had it but
you lost it for both of us. You were too
slow. But you saw me. I was right
there with it. I was in masterpiece
mode until you fucked it up. Maybe
next time you'll remember how kick
ass I was and you'll follow along like I
tell you. If we're going to be in a band
together then we have to work
together and you'll have to learn to
do what I tell you FASTER!

KG looks sorry.

**KG**
I want to write a masterpiece, dude.

JB sits down defeated.

**JB**
Me too dude. We've just got writers block. It happens to the best of them.

JB picks up some of the Rolling Stone magazines that lay on the floor around him. He looks longingly at their covers.

**JB**
I mean look at these guys... AC/DC, Van Halen, The Who! Why are you guys so awesome? What do you have that we don't have!?

JB puts his head into his hands. KG picks up the magazines and glances at them.

**KG**
(under his breath)
Well... They all use the same guitar pick.

JB snaps to attention.

**JB**
What?

**KG**
It's probably nothing. I'm just saying, they all got the same guitar pick. See.

JB comes to his side and looks at the covers KG is holding.

Three extreme zooms focus tight on different Rolling Stone covers. There is the same strange guitar pick in each of the different musicians' hands. This small detail would only be noticeable with a magnifying glass.

The D exchange a look of amazement and fear.

**JB**
Holy shit balls.

You soon learned the amazing history of this strange pick, the P.O.D. — the Pick of Destiny itself — when you visited the Guitar Center Music Store, and met the manager there, a hardened ex-roadie named Sebastian who had spent years researching it . Now obviously the true identity of 'Sebastian' is a closely guarded secret...

**Kyle:** Yeah, he's not even really called Sebastian.

**... but in the movie he's portrayed by Ben Stiller. He was in the video for 'Tribute', so presumably he's a 'friend of the band'. How was it like working with him again?**

**Jack:** He brought the thunder, to say the least... We needed someone to bring the thick and juicy, fuckin' *gravitas*.

**Kyle:** It was a difficult part and he came through with aplomb.

**Jack:** He has to lay out the whole story of the pick. There was a lot of pressure on him to throw down, and he felt it too.

**Kyle:** When he was preparing, he didn't come out of his trailer for thirteen hours.

**Jack:** It's true.

**What was he doing in there for all that time?**

**Kyle:** It's hard to know for certain 'cos there was no one else in there. Maybe yoga positions.

**Jack:** He was experiencing an emotional upheaval at the magnitude of his task. But he came on set, and he nailed it. He brung it. He rung that bell two times!

# IDENTITY CONCEALED FOR SECURITY REASONS

*What you seek my friends... is the Pick of Destiny...*

'Sebastian'
Guitar Center Manager /
Hardened Ex-Roadie

# TOP SECRET

FROM THE RESEARCH NOTES OF SEBASTIAN:

It is the darkest secret in the history of rock.

I actually saw it once... on the road. I used to be the most sought-after guitar tech in the business. I even had groupies... which is extremely uncommon for a guitar tech. Then one night I was working this job – I saw this guitarist play some shit that was way beyond his capabilities. I noticed he was using a new guitar pick. That had to be it, but he didn't know what he had. At the end of the show he flicked it into the audience. A kid caught it. A kid named Eddie.

Eddie Van Halen.

I started researching it. Turns out this thing goes deeper than I could have imagined. Back before rock and roll. Back to the Dark Ages. I quit my job, went to Rome and lived there for three years. Learned Latin. I gained the trust of the Night Librarian at the Vatican. A gentleman by the name of Salvatore Papardello. He turned me on to some shit you wouldn't believe.

Long ago, a dark Wizard used his black magic to summon Satan himself.

But the great Demon was far too powerful. A horrific battle ensued.

# The Legend of the Pick of Destiny

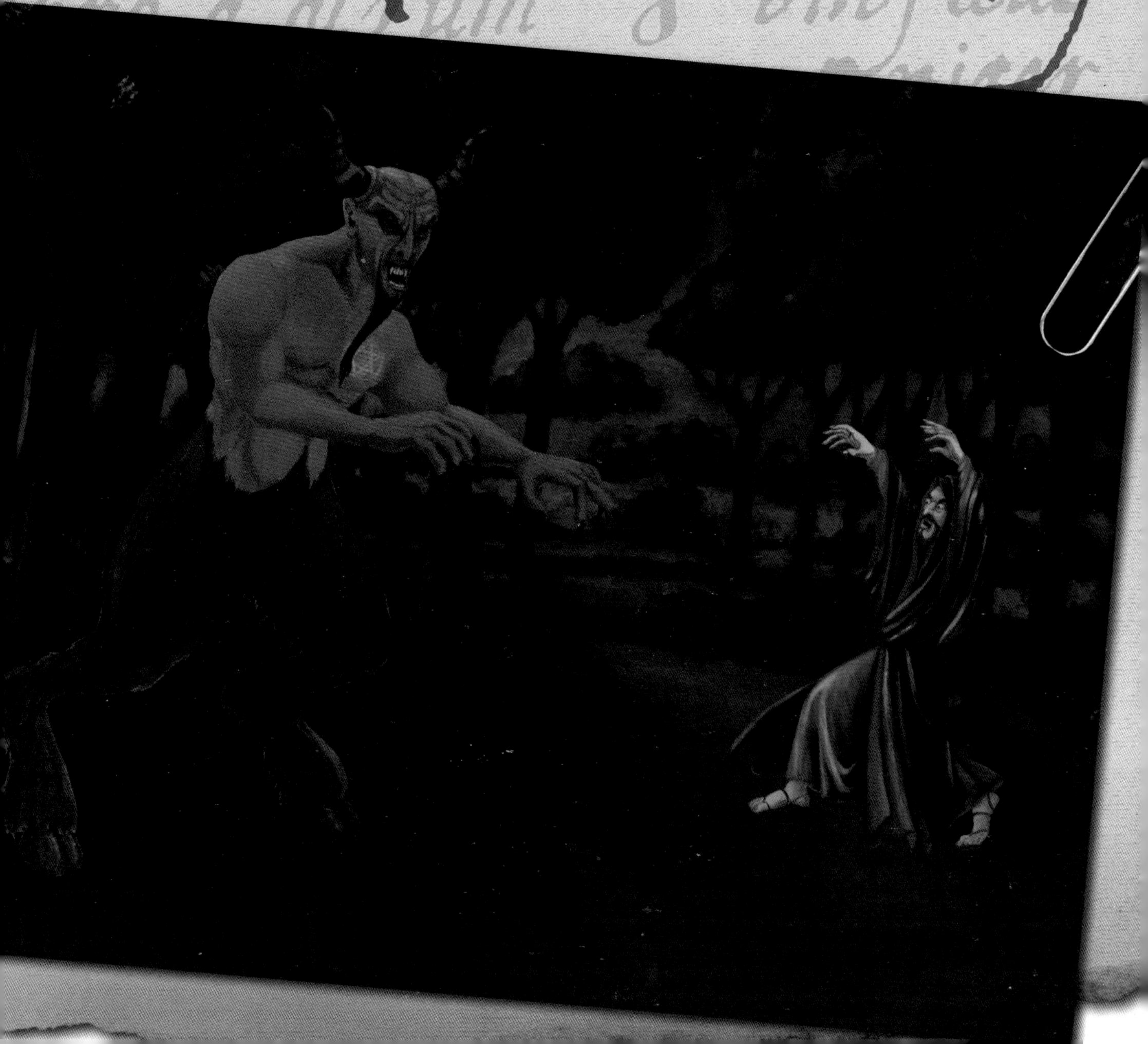

Luckily, a Blacksmith and friend to the Wizard, heard the beast's roars... and hurled a horseshoe at the Demon's face, chipping his front tooth.

"AHHH! FUCK! YOU CHIPPED MY TOOTH! WHERE is it? I am not COMPLETE!"

The Wizard looked down and saw the shard of tooth near his foot. He placed his foot over it to hide it from view. Taking advantage of the Demon's moment of vulnerability, the Wizard then whispered a softly spoken magic spell.

In loco unde venisti
Remanebis
Donec denuo completus sis.

TRANSLATION:
From whence you came
You shall remain
Until you are complete again.

The Demon was drawn back into the fires of hell and the dark Wizard was totally stoked to be alive. With a long draw on his hash pipe the Wizard devised a way to repay the Blacksmith.

The Wizard knew that the Blacksmith loved a fair maiden. Yet she was unimpressed with his crude profession. To gain her affection, the Blacksmith would need a true master's skill that would leave the maiden's vagina moist and wanting.

And so the Wizard fashioned the Demon's tooth into a pick...

...A pick that would make the Blacksmith play only the most masterful of melodies on his lute... thereby winning the heart of the maiden he loved.

The secret of the pick died with the Blacksmith, but over time, it passed through many hands. Mozart had it... How do you think he busted out all those classical jams? Then it was gone... poof. It disappeared for centuries. Then, bang... it shows up in the United States at the turn of the century and spawns the blues and rock n' roll. I traced it back to England where it sparked the British Invasion... punk, new wave, metal... The pick wasn't following the music, the music was following the pick.

WOLFGANG AMADEUS MOZART

Who had the P.O.D.?

Mozart
Benjamin Franklin
Einstein
Robert Johnson
John Lee Hooker
Brian Jones
John Lennon
JFK
Jimmy Page
Johnny Ramone
Tony Iommi
Stan Lee
Leonard Nimoy
Ron Silver
Stephen Hawking
Eddie Van Halen
Angus Young

**We know Mozart had it the pick, and that it was later owned by Eddie Van Halen and Angus Young: is anything else known about who else had the Pick of Destiny?**
**Jack:** I know who had it and who didn't. Einstein had it. Benjamin Franklin had it. JFK had it. Lots of fuckers had it. It wasn't just rock. It was inspiration to be rocking. Name some people you think were kick-ass, in the history of the world — most of the top people had it.

It's a tiny piece of the beast himself so it has supernatural — supra-natural — qualities.

The last time it was photographed was with one of Angus Young's guitars. This guitar was later sold at an auction and ended up in the Rock and Roll History Museum.

My guess is that the P.O.D. must have gone with it.

BENJAMIN FRANKLIN

The QUEST.

"When we get that fucking pick... we're going to dominate the world of rock!"

INT. ARMY SURPLUS STORE

                JB
Dude, getting this pick is not going to be
easy. It's gonna be a major fucking heist
and we're not going to be able to do it
without the proper equipment!

                KG
Word.

*Shopping List*
Night vision goggles
Two skin-tight camouflage
    jumpsuits
Crossbow grappling hook with
    retract-o action
Fifteen inch Bowie knife with
    compass in the handle
Dog whistles
Diamond tipped glass cutter
Water-proof matches
Num chucks
Blow darts with horse
    tranquilizer tips
Twelve suction cups
Tear gas
Flare gun
Bungee cord
One bag of Funyuns (for KG)
Walkie talkies

        SURPLUS STORE CLERK
Looks to me like you fellers might be
fixin' to take the law into your own
hands...

                KG
No. Just going on a little camping trip.

        SURPLUS STORE CLERK
Alls I'm saying is some people might
think you're planning to overthrow the
government...
        (leaning in, discrete, creepy)
and some of *us* folks might give you a
thumbs up... a *big* thumbs up... WAY up...

        SURPLUS STORE CLERK
That'll be one thousand six hundred
and eighty-two dollars.

                KG
I believe the num chucks are on sale.

        SURPLUS STORE CLERK
Naw, that was last month...

                JB
...How much for just the walkie talkies?

        SURPLUS STORE CLERK
Ninety-nine, ninety-nine.

JB pulls KG aside.

                JB
Dude, how much do you have?

                KG
I've only got twenty bucks.

                JB
        (angry)
You've only got twenty bucks?! Fuck!
Fuck! Fuck!

                KG
Do we really need walkie talkies?

                JB
Of course we fucking need them! It's the
only way to triangulate our mission
objectives!

                KG
Looks like it's time to rock our way out
of a tight situation...

                JB
Let's blow this freak's mind with a tailor
made jam.

**Tell us about the song you came up with to get you those free walkie talkies.**

Jack: Well, it was cut from the film actually — look for it on the DVD extras! But it's on the album. It's our battle cry against the oppressive, ignorant religious stupidity that rules our land presently.

**It's impressive: a spontaneous 'tailor-made jam'. Can the D just pull one of those out of the bag whenever needed?**
Kyle: When we're up against it we can do anything.
Jack: Hence the training. That's the discipline.

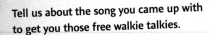

## SURPLUS STORE CLERK

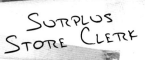

The surplus store clerk has a tear in his eye as he hands over the walkie talkies.

SURPLUS STORE CLERK
These ones is on the house.

# The Government Totally Sucks

The government totally sucks, you motherfucker
The government totally sucks.

The government totally sucks, you motherfucker
The government totally sucks.

Hey!

Ben Franklin was a rebel indeed,
He liked to get naked while he smoked on the weed.
He was a genius, but if he was here today
The government would fuck him up his righteous A!

Now let me tell you something 'bout the government,
They're fucking up the environment.

They're taking all the beautiful fucking animals (Yeah?)
And making them fucking extinct! (Oh no!)

The government totally sucks, you motherfucker
The government totally sucks.
The government totally sucks.

'Cause the land of love and freedom
Is just a baby's breath away.
And if we hold hands together,
We can bring back the USA.

The USA-AAA yeah
The USA-AAA yeah
The fuckin' USA-AAA yeah

Bring back the US -

Government totally sucks!

You borrowed Lee's car, telling him you needed it to get to a meeting with the president of a record label, and hit the road, on your epic quest to find the pick at the Rock and Roll Museum. Speaking of which, what's it like on 'the road' when the D are on tour? Fucking tough? An absence of guff?

**Jack:** The road is glorious, yet treacherous. You gotta be ready to leave your loved ones behind and maybe never see them again.

**Kyle:** Travelling around in a luxury bus with satellite TV? It's hell.

Back to the quest: as KG was driving, you drifted into a reverie JB, and dreamt of what might be... Tell us about 'Master Exploder'.

**Jack:** Simple. If there was a question: What if we rocked even harder than we already rock? This song is the answer.

---

INT. OPEN MIC NIGHT – JACK'S DREAM

Paul F. Tompkins takes the stage.

OPEN MIC HOST
Ladies and gentlemen, the band you are about to see asked me not to read this. But, godammit I'm going to read it because I wrote it and it's the truth.
(looking to index card, reading)
I fucking love this band. They are the best band ever, period. Ladies and gentlemen, Tenacious D.

The crowd cheers as KG and JB take the stage.

JB wears a green pick on the end of a tight necklace.

JB
(whispered)
Hey what's up. We're Tenacious D. Sometimes inspiration creeps up on you. Me and KG wrote this song five minutes ago... It's called Master Exploder.

HIT IT KAGE.

I DO NOT NEED A MIC. MY VOICE IS SO

I'M SORRY. I DIDN'T MEAN TO BLOW YOUR MIND. THIS KIND OF SHIT HAPPENS TO ME ALL THE TIME!

INT. TRUCK STOP DINER

KG

What's the matter? Aren't you hungry, man? You should eat something.

JB

I never eat before a mission. It makes you slow. I got to stay light on my feet. Like a dancer... Like a ninja. Now check this out.

JB takes the Rock and Roll Museum brochure and grabs a napkin. He begins drawing a map.

KG

I've been thinking. I don't know about this late night break in idea... Maybe we should just go there while it's open, I create a distraction, and you snag it when no one's looking...

JB

No. We've got to go at night! In the secrecy of the shadows! Stealth is our ally! You think we can just walk in and ask them if they'll give us the fucking Pick of Destiny? We just need a plan, now look at this...

JB starts drawing diagrams of a plan. As he whispers the plan, KG notices some cute ladies sitting at a booth smiling at him. JB continues explaining his plan but KG is too distracted by the girls at the table. He flirts with them. JB realizes KG isn't focused on his plan and starts getting angry.

JB (cont'd)

God damn it Kyle, if we're going to do this you have got to be focused. Eye of le Tigra. Now check this out... if we shimmy up this and go around back and look for the...

KG
(interrupts)

Hold on a sec.

KG gets up and goes to the booth where the ladies are sitting. JB's anger makes him more determined to finish his plans.

**On the way to the Rock and Roll History museum, you stopped off at a diner. JB 'never eats before a mission', but how important is food to the D?**

**Kyle:** Food is crucial. In fact, it's interesting, I just started eating right as you asked that question! Food nourishes us. It inspires us. Satisfies us. Food also provides us with love. It feels the same or better than actual love. That's why food is so important.

**Jack:** Eating, fucking, and shitting — the holy trinity of life's great pleasures. See, eating's right up there with fucking and shitting!

**So what kind of food is on the D's backstage rider?**

**Jack:** We invented this one. It's called the King Henry the Eighth Backstage Rider. We just go: mutton chops, big bowl o' grapes, a flagon of wine. We put only stuff King Henry the Eighth himself stuffed down his tasty gullet. I saw his backstage rider, and we just copied it. It was at a TV studio.

**Kyle:** The only difference is that we threw in Power Bars, and that's it.

**Jack:** Power Bars — that's the only thing he didn't have back in the day.

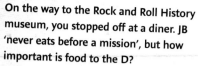

KING HENRY VIII

I LOVE YA BABY BUT ALL I CAN THINK ABOUT IS KIELBASA SAUSAGE

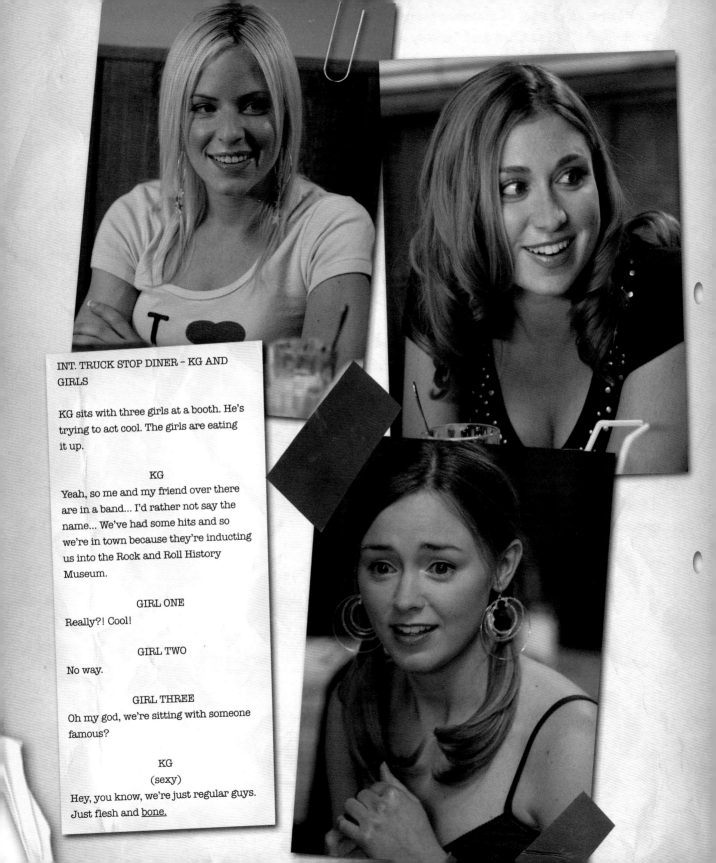

INT. TRUCK STOP DINER – KG AND
GIRLS

KG sits with three girls at a booth. He's
trying to act cool. The girls are eating
it up.

KG
Yeah, so me and my friend over there
are in a band... I'd rather not say the
name... We've had some hits and so
we're in town because they're inducting
us into the Rock and Roll History
Museum.

GIRL ONE
Really?! Cool!

GIRL TWO
No way.

GIRL THREE
Oh my god, we're sitting with someone
famous?

KG
(sexy)
Hey, you know, we're just regular guys.
Just flesh and bone.

**KG was somewhat distracted from the mission by the girls in the diner... What are the D's views on groupies?**
Kyle: Well, groupies are like temptresses. They're very tempting to dip into but you gotta watch your step. It could be a quagmire because they might not really know you, or indeed actually like you.
Jack: They are just lonely travellers looking for joy from the loins of the gods.

**And you are the gods?**
Jack: We try to tell them we are mere mortals, but they *will not listen*! They sucketh upon the mushroom cap and stroketh upon the shaft... and if perchance the mayonnaise of love doth spray upon mine brow, looketh upon me kindly for I am a gentle soul at heart.

**And 'pleasing' the ladies in general: any tips on technique?**
Kyle: Well, I think the key to any fulfilling and satisfying sex life is friction. Not much, a little. It's all about friction really.
Jack: [sings] I need a little friiiictiooooon! Dude, we should write a song about friction!
Kyle: Yup, because if you think about it —
Jack: That's all it comes down to? Ah, but it's not all friction. It's also a hot moisture. Heat and moisture are fucking just as important as friction.
Kyle: But doesn't the heat come from the friction?
Jack: Not necessarily, dude. If you pour some fucking hot gravy on my cock, that shit is gonna feel goooood!
Kyle: Hot gravy!?
Jack: I don't want *you* to pour it on there. But look, here's what I'm gonna

say: focus on their beauty, but relish your own pleasure first and foremost. She wants you to nut your brains out, that shit turns her *on*. The end.

**Awesome. But there's one thing we *need* to know: if you're 'double teaming', how does the side-hatch fit in?**
Kyle: I'm afraid the side-hatch is just a metaphor. It doesn't really exist.

**Any 'tools' you'd recommend? A feather and French tickler, perhaps?**
Kyle: I recommend The Bullet. I think a very compact vibrator, used sparingly, can bring a woman to ecstasy. Now, I've had to use one for years because my equipment stopped working properly...
Jack: I'd say that all tools are fair game.

**All tools?**
Jack: *All* tools.

INT. TRUCK STOP DINER

STRANGER
I've tried to get the Pick of Destiny. I had it in my hands too... but I was caught. Triggered a laser and a security door came down on my leg. Cut it right off... I did three years in the slammer but I'd do it all again if I still had my leg. Yeah, my criminal days are through. Man, I miss that sweet ass leg of mine...

JB interrupts.

JB
Why are you telling me this?!

STRANGER
I like you. You got that spark in your eye that I once had. The dream. The dream of harnessing that power in the name of rock. Now, look at my plans. They'll help you I promise. There's two air ducts on the roof. That's where you'll go in.

JB's encounter with the seedy Stranger, who seems to know a lot about the P.O.D., is recreated in the movie with Tim Robbins portraying the Stranger. What was it like working with him?

**Kyle:** Well, Tim's an old buddy. We go way back with Tim. So it was just like having an old friend around really. Very familiar. Normally he would be directing us though, so it was nice to be able to tell him what to do.

**Jack:** Yeah. The shoe was on the other foot!

**Kyle:** It was the first time he was sorta working for us. So we *relished* the opportunity to give him notes on his performance, tell him where to stand and why. But he did a great job, so we were thankful.

**Jack:** Tim goes where few actors are willing to go when creating a character. Look for him come Oscar time on this one.

INT. TRUCK STOP DINER

**KG**
Dude! I got some smokin' Betties over there and they want us to play a gig!

**JB**
No. Listen to me. I just had the weirdest conversation in my life. This dude just gave me the perfect plan. It's a fucking sign! We are surrounded by ancient forces here! We can do this. Check it out, there are two air ducts on the roof...

JB tries to show him the new napkin but KG looks at the babes in the booth.

**KG**
But dude, the party and getting to play our tunes, *AND* I think that one hottie wants to ride my wrinkle stick!

JB looks him in the eye.

**JB**
Would you get your head out of the fucking pussy clouds, man! Who gives a shit about these chicks?! There's going to be ten times hotter babes backstage when we win album of the year! That pick is our ticket to genius!

KG looks over to the ladies and waves as if everything is fine.

**KG**
Dude. I can't believe you'd skip a gig opportunity with some sweet-ass hotties to do this. Is this thing really that important to you? I mean, we can still write a masterpiece and win that dough. Maybe we just need more practice? Did you ever think of that? Maybe The D would be bet-ter if we just worked on our songwriting instead of relying on ancient bullshit that probably won't work anyway!

**JB**
Well, what's it gonna be dude? You have to decide, Tits... Or Destiny!

**KG**
I'm going to have to go with tits.

KG walks away towards the babes in the booth. JB is left standing alone. JB walks slowly to the door talking loud enough for KG to hear. He makes a scene out of his exit.

**JB**
Um... Good luck buddy! I hope it was worth it! We're done! You ruined it! The pick's mine! I don't need you! I don't fucking need you! Later, cock ass!

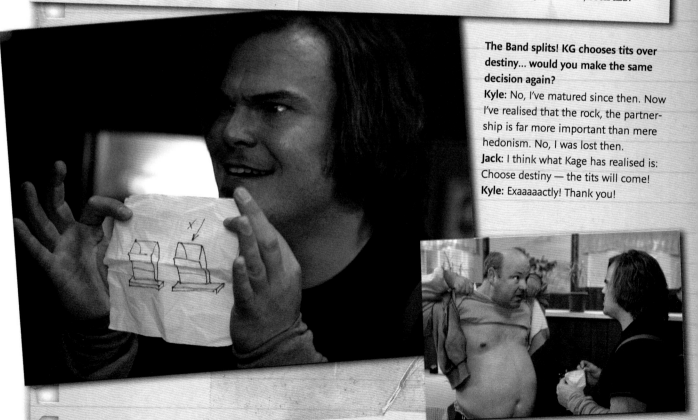

**The Band splits! KG chooses tits over destiny... would you make the same decision again?**
**Kyle:** No, I've matured since then. Now I've realised that the rock, the partnership is far more important than mere hedonism. No, I was lost then.
**Jack:** I think what Kage has realised is: Choose destiny — the tits will come!
**Kyle:** Exaaaaactly! Thank you!

The DIVIDE.

"You're saying hoes before bros.
Well that's not how I roll asshole."

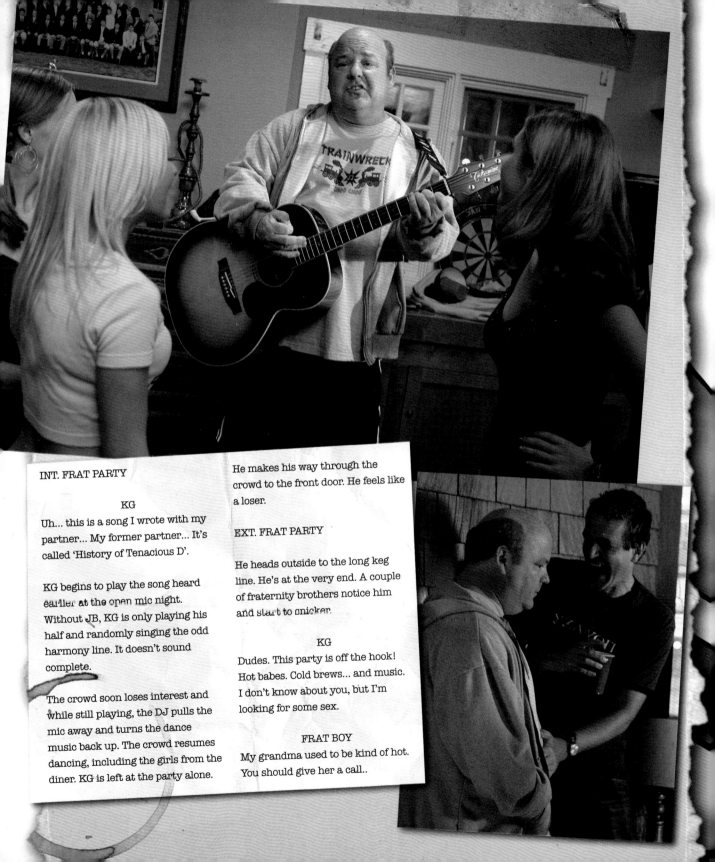

INT. FRAT PARTY

KG
Uh... this is a song I wrote with my partner... My former partner... It's called 'History of Tenacious D'.

KG begins to play the song heard earlier at the open mic night. Without JB, KG is only playing his half and randomly singing the odd harmony line. It doesn't sound complete.

The crowd soon loses interest and while still playing, the DJ pulls the mic away and turns the dance music back up. The crowd resumes dancing, including the girls from the diner. KG is left at the party alone.

He makes his way through the crowd to the front door. He feels like a loser.

EXT. FRAT PARTY

He heads outside to the long keg line. He's at the very end. A couple of fraternity brothers notice him and start to snicker.

KG
Dudes. This party is off the hook! Hot babes. Cold brews... and music. I don't know about you, but I'm looking for some sex.

FRAT BOY
My grandma used to be kind of hot. You should give her a call..

EXT. DARK FOREST – NIGHT

JB is sitting on the ground leaning against a tree trunk. He's picking and eating wild mushrooms from a patch beside him. His shirt is covered in mushroom stems as he eats.

JB
(still mad)
It's a good thing I found these mushrooms! I was fucking starving...

JB stands and brushes the mushroom crumbs off of his shirt and pants. He looks a bit dazed.

JB
This place is kind of... juicy.

EXT. DARK FOREST – NIGHT

Through a clearing JB sees Sasquatch walking by exactly like the classic Bigfoot footage. JB points and yells.

JB
Oh my god! Sasquatch!

Sasquatch stops in mid-stride and turns. He smiles broadly, at once recognizing it's JB.

SASQUATCH
Jables! What's up?

JB runs over to Sasquatch.

JB
(dreamy, glee)
I was just walking through your beautiful forest.

SASQUATCH
It's not my forest brother. It's everyone's.

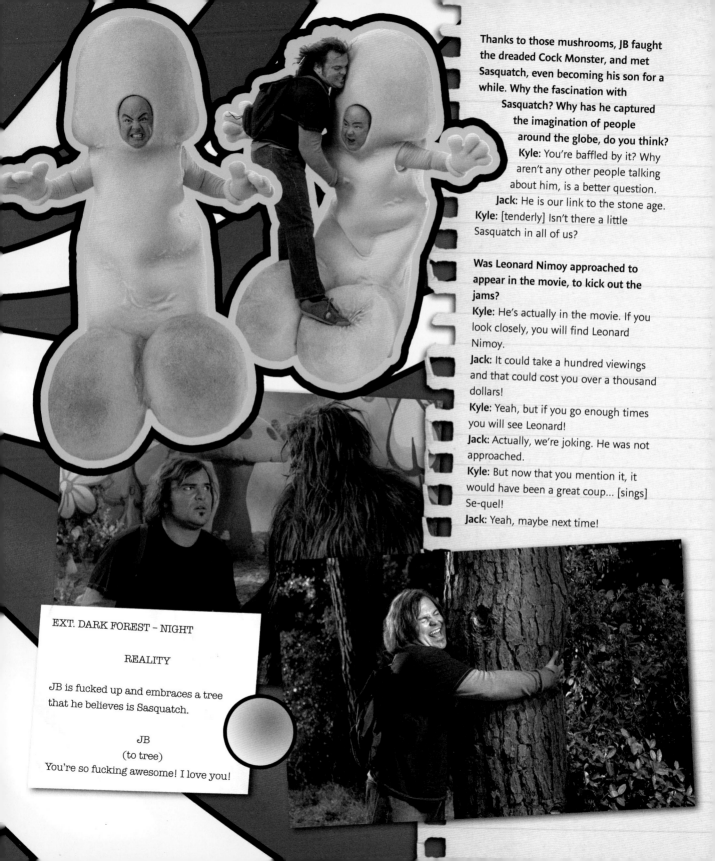

Thanks to those mushrooms, JB faught the dreaded Cock Monster, and met Sasquatch, even becoming his son for a while. Why the fascination with Sasquatch? Why has he captured the imagination of people around the globe, do you think?

Kyle: You're baffled by it? Why aren't any other people talking about him, is a better question.

Jack: He is our link to the stone age.

Kyle: [tenderly] Isn't there a little Sasquatch in all of us?

**Was Leonard Nimoy approached to appear in the movie, to kick out the jams?**

Kyle: He's actually in the movie. If you look closely, you will find Leonard Nimoy.

Jack: It could take a hundred viewings and that could cost you over a thousand dollars!

Kyle: Yeah, but if you go enough times you will see Leonard!

Jack: Actually, we're joking. He was not approached.

Kyle: But now that you mention it, it would have been a great coup... [sings] Se-quel!

Jack: Yeah, maybe next time!

EXT. DARK FOREST – NIGHT

REALITY

JB is fucked up and embraces a tree that he believes is Sasquatch.

JB
(to tree)
You're so fucking awesome! I love you!

EXT. FRAT PARTY – LATER

KG is nearly at the keg. The frat guys that made fun of him have just finished filling their cups. They walk away laughing.

FRAT BOY

Later, Grampa.

KG ignores them and attempts to fill his cup, but the keg is empty. All that's left is runny foam. He walks away dejectedly staring at the beer foam in his cup. The scene plays out to the song, 'Dude I Totally Miss You'.

As KG stares, the foam in his cup becomes a looking glass of his good memories with JB.

In the foam he sees some touching moments from their past.

## Dude I Totally Miss You

Dude, I totally miss you
Really fuckin' miss you.
I'm all alone all the time, all the time.
Dude I totally miss you
Things we did together.
Where have you gone?

Totally miss the honesty
and special times,
And honestly, totally miss the fucked
up things you do.

Dude, I totally miss you
I totally miss you
Dude, I totally miss you all the time.

Totally miss the honesty
and special times,
And honestly, totally miss the fucked
up things you do.

Dude, I totally miss you
I totally miss you
Dude, I totally miss you all the time.

All the time.

**Tell us about 'Dude I Totally Miss You'. It's a touching paean from one band member to another...**

**Kyle:** It's probably the most touching song ever written.

**Jack:** Yeah. We wanted to write a ballad for the ages. I just remember saying to Kage, 'Kage, play the saddest fucking chord you know of.' And he played a chord and I said, '*Dig deeper!* Find an even more painful chord!' And then he played a chord that wasn't painful at all and I said, 'C'mon, get serious!' And then he fuckin' found it! What was the final chord you ended on?

**Kyle:** I think it was an E minor.

**Jack:** Yeah, and it was *heartbreaking*. And then it just spilled forth.

EXT. THE ROCK AND ROLL
MUSEUM – NIGHT

JB is crouched behind some bushes and
makes a dash across a parking lot
towards the museum.

He does a stealthy crouch run into a
diving somersault and stands with his
back flat against the brick exterior of
the museum. He sidesteps out of frame.

JB is pumped up on adrenaline. His back
is still pressed flat against the wall. He
comes to the wall's end and does a quick
check around the corner, noticing a sur-
veillance camera mounted on the wall.

He picks up a stone while in the
middle of a ninja-like roll. He dives

while throwing the rock and
knocks out the security camera.
He continues running.

JB pulls himself onto the rooftop. He
is immediately stealthy. He crouch
runs with eyes darting.

With fast slamming zooms, JB notices
another security camera monitoring
the roof.

CUT TO:

INT. MUSEUM SECURITY CENTER

Two security guards are talking.
They don't notice JB doing a cartwheel through the frame of the
rooftop security monitor.

CUT TO:

EXT. MUSEUM ROOFTOP

JB comes out of his cartwheel and notices the two air ducts in front of him. He crouch runs to them and rips the metal grating off of one. JB does a running dive into the open air duct. There are a couple beats of silence then the echoing crash of him landing two stories down inside the air duct.

**JB, after your side 'trip' with Sasquatch, you made your way to the Rock and Roll Museum, and displayed some impressive ninja skills as you broke in. Where did you learn them?**
**Jack:** I am a ninja. End of that question. No, where did I learn my skills? From a another ninja. An older ninja. And that's all I can say. I am forbidden to discuss such matters with non-ninjas.

INT. MUSEUM AIR DUCT

JB's upside down and bent in an uncomfortable cramped space within the duct. He rolls over and begins to crawl. He rants.

JB
Ugh. That was fucking KG's fault. If he had been here like we planned he could have lowered me down with a rope but dickass had to follow his cock. And you know when I go quadruple plat he'll come a knockin', "Hey dude, can I come back in your band now?" And I'll be like, "Fuck you, Cockshiner."

JB comes to a wider section of air duct. To his left a large fan slowly spins. He crawls into the new section and heads to the right.

JB
And he'll be like, "You need to loosen up and smell the roses, man." And I'll be like, "Yeah, I'll fucking smell the roses cuz' I'm headlining at the fucking Rose Bowl tomorrow, bitch ass. Motherfucker."

And he'll be like...

KG's voice is heard coming from JB's walkie talkie. JB mistakes it for the KG in his head.

KG (Off Screen)
Hey, dude. Can you hear me?

JB
And I'll be like, "Oh, yeah I hear you loud and clear. You're saying hoes before bros. Well that's not how I roll asshole."

KG (O.S.)
Dude!

JB
Don't you "dude" me. Only dudes call me dude!

KG (O.S.)
(interrupts)
JB it's KG do you read me?

JB realizes KG's voice is coming from his walkie talkie. He fishes it out of his backpack and presses its button.

JB
(into walkie talkie)
What the fuck do you want, NON-rocker? This line is reserved for rockers only! So I can't really talk to you right now!

KG (O.S.)
Dude, where are you? Are you in the museum?

JB
What do you care, ex-friend? So you shot your load and now you want to come back to The D? Well, while you were spritzing on fannies I've been cranking out Grammys. You blew it. Check mate. I win.

KG (O.S.)
Dude, "Sex, Drugs AND THEN Rock and Roll". In that order. I was just following the code.

JB comes to a grating in the air duct looking down over the museum. He notices a security guard walking below him. He watches him through the grate.

JB
(angry whisper)
You're a fucking traitor! You bailed on me and now I'm in the shit and where the fuck are you?

The shot reveals KG in the air duct directly in front of JB. He's holding the other walkie talkie in his hand. JB hasn't noticed him. He speaks without the walkie talkie.

KG
I'm in the air duct, dude.

JB looks up at him. They stare at each other for a couple of seconds.

**KG**

Dude. I totally missed you.

**JB**

Me too.

Suddenly the section of air duct they are in gives way from their combined weight. The section crashes to the floor with them inside it.

CUT TO:

INT. ROCK AND ROLL MUSEUM – CLASSIC ROCK DISPLAY ROOM

An eight foot section of duct lays on the ground. KG and JB's heads slowly come out from each end of it looking directly to camera.

**Tenacious D are masters of cursing. Are you proud of bringing new terms into the language, such as 'cock ass'? And indeed, 'cockshiner'?**

**Jack:** Not to mention the never-before-heard 'cocksqueezer'.

**Kyle:** Ooh.

**Jack:** And fuck-a-luck-a-ding-dong! Yes, there is a sense of accomplishment when you invent new contributions to the nation's lexicon.

**What are the best swearwords, or constructions, in the D's opinion?**

**Jack:** I feel there's one classic one, which just fits together like a fuckin' terrific choo-choo train of profanity. It's not that it's extra bad, but when you put all these words together they sound right to me: goddamnmutherfuckinstoopidpieceofshit! It has a poetry to it: *goddamn-mutherfuckinstoopidpieceofshit!* See what I mean?

**Kyle:** It has a good rhythm to it...

**Jack:** Which is why it's also a new song we wrote that we haven't released yet. [sings] Goddamnmutherfuckinstoopidpieceofshit! Goddamnmutherfuckinstoopidpieceofshit!

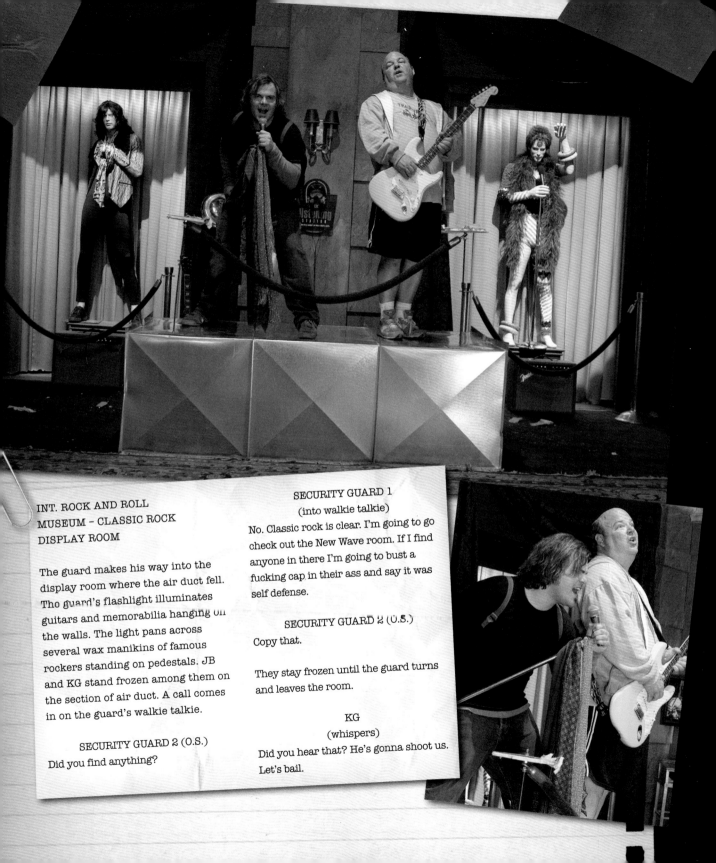

INT. ROCK AND ROLL
MUSEUM – CLASSIC ROCK
DISPLAY ROOM

The guard makes his way into the
display room where the air duct fell.
The guard's flashlight illuminates
guitars and memorabilia hanging on
the walls. The light pans across
several wax manikins of famous
rockers standing on pedestals. JB
and KG stand frozen among them on
the section of air duct. A call comes
in on the guard's walkie talkie.

SECURITY GUARD 2 (O.S.)
Did you find anything?

SECURITY GUARD 1
(into walkie talkie)
No. Classic rock is clear. I'm going to go
check out the New Wave room. If I find
anyone in there I'm going to bust a
fucking cap in their ass and say it was
self defense.

SECURITY GUARD 2 (O.S.)
Copy that.

They stay frozen until the guard turns
and leaves the room.

KG
(whispers)
Did you hear that? He's gonna shoot us.
Let's bail.

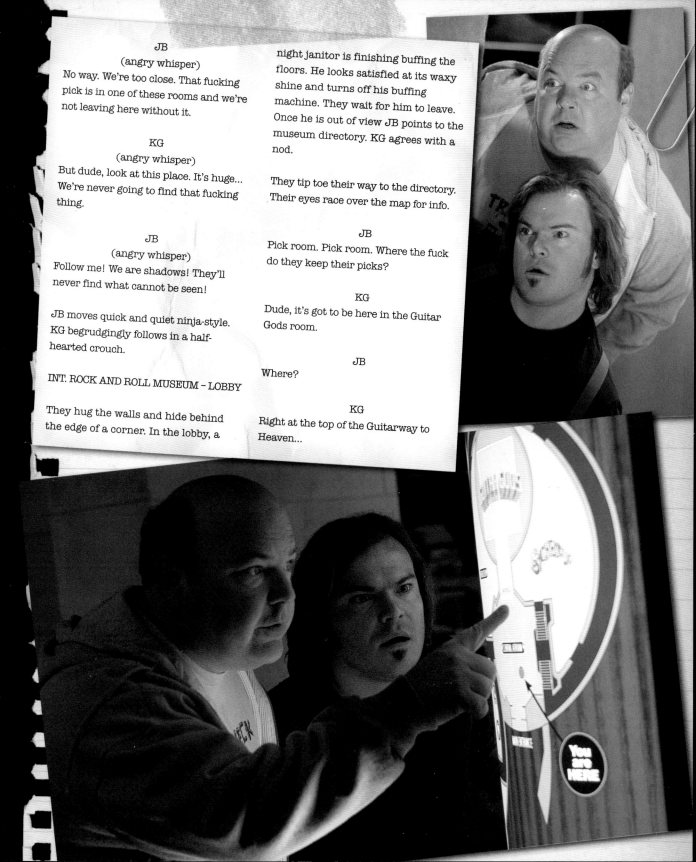

JB
(angry whisper)
No way. We're too close. That fucking pick is in one of these rooms and we're not leaving here without it.

KG
(angry whisper)
But dude, look at this place. It's huge... We're never going to find that fucking thing.

JB
(angry whisper)
Follow me! We are shadows! They'll never find what cannot be seen!

JB moves quick and quiet ninja-style. KG begrudgingly follows in a half-hearted crouch.

INT. ROCK AND ROLL MUSEUM - LOBBY

They hug the walls and hide behind the edge of a corner. In the lobby, a night janitor is finishing buffing the floors. He looks satisfied at its waxy shine and turns off his buffing machine. They wait for him to leave. Once he is out of view JB points to the museum directory. KG agrees with a nod.

They tip toe their way to the directory. Their eyes race over the map for info.

JB
Pick room. Pick room. Where the fuck do they keep their picks?

KG
Dude, it's got to be here in the Guitar Gods room.

JB
Where?

KG
Right at the top of the Guitarway to Heaven...

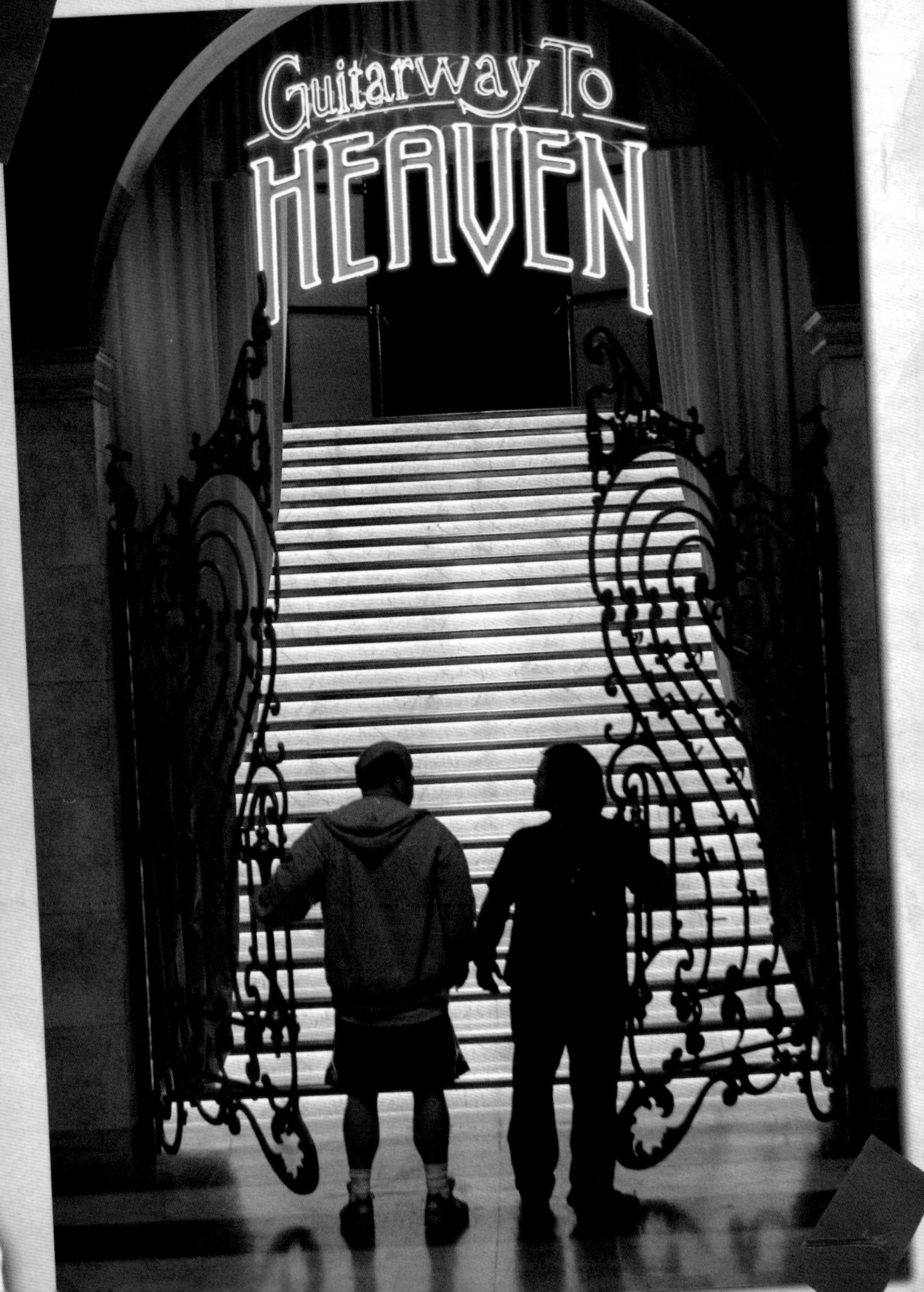
Guitarway To
HEAVEN

INT. GUITAR GOD ROOM ENTRANCE

                    JB
Fuck-a-luck-a-ding-dong.

                    KG
               (salivating)
Let's get it.

KG starts walking towards the pick.

JB grabs him before he can enter the
room.

                    JB
No! Lasers... They'll cut you to pieces.
Sizzleen. You stay here and keep a look
out.

                    KG
What are you gonna do?

                    JB
Time to thread the needle my friend.
I'm going in there and getting that pick.

INT. GUITAR GOD ROOM

JB unhooks a red velvet rope blocking
the doorway. He enters the laser grid
sideways so he can fit between the
first set of beams. He pivots on the

spot, squats and does a tight
somersault that leads into a bunny-
hop. He nails a one footed landing
while holding his left knee to his
chest. A laser beam runs a millimeter
under his left foot.

                    JB
               (to himself)
Jackknife.

His face shows all the intensity of a bullfighter in a hurricane.

INT. GUITAR GOD ROOM ENTRANCE

KG watches nervously. He is sweating.

KG
(whispered)
You got it buddy. You're gonna make it...

INT. GUITAR GOD ROOM

The laser beams grow denser as JB makes his way closer to the guitars. He is sweating.

JB now has his back against the side wall. He lays down and pushes off the wall with his feet, sliding on his stomach under several low laser beams. He rolls over two times and then crouches into a tight cannon ball and tippy toes through a small opening in the grid.

CUT TO:

INT. GUITAR GOD ROOM ENTRANCE

KG is sweating more.

KG
(whispered)
You got it. You're almost there!

CUT TO:

INT. GUITAR GOD ROOM

JB is frozen in a tangled web of lasers. His arms are over his head in a ridiculously awkward pose.

JB
Can't reach pick... surrounded by lasers...

KG (O.S.)
(angry whisper)
Focus Jables! Use all your mental powers!

JB
Wait! There's a button down here... I think it might deactivate the lasers. But I can't reach it...

CLOSE UP OF SECURITY SYSTEM SWITCH

The wall mounted switch has two buttons. It stands a foot away at crotch level. JB can not lower his arms or move.

CUT TO:

INT. GUITAR GOD ROOM ENTRANCE

KG looks determined.

KG
(intense whisper)
The cock...

CLOSE UP OF KG'S FACE

KG
Use the cock!

Reunited, you made your way up the Guitarway to Heaven to the Guitar Gods room, where you finally found the Pick of Destiny. You made some tricksy maneuvers through those lasers, JB. How did it feel to save the day with your cock?

**Jack:** The training was all worth it. It felt good *on* the cock!

**Kyle:** What did you think of, to get that cock so hard?

**Jack:** It was actually an absence of thought. I wasn't thinking of porno or anything like that, because when you have to use the cock in that way it's not really about being turned on. It's about mind over boner.

Can you assure us that no special effects were involved? That there was no stunt cock used?

**Jack:** That was one thousand per cent Jack Black cock!

**Kyle:** And it was one take!

What exactly is the reach of your cock?

**Jack:** Well, I don't have one of those two hander porno cocks, where the woman has to use two hands to stroke it correctly. But my cock does feel really good when it is being stroked, or sucked or caressed or whatever. So I know that it works good. That's the most important thing, right? Feels good? *Yeah*. In that

respect, the cock is one of the best cocks in history.

Does anyone in rock have a longer cock-reach than you?

**Kyle:** I think Robert Plant looks like he's packing some heat.

**Jack:** Robert Plant?

**Kyle:** His jeans are kinda faded in the cock region.

**Jack:** But the thing is that Robert Plant is probably like four feet tall, weighs 89 pounds. So a little cock is gonna go a *loooong* way on a little guy like that.

**Kyle:** You're saying it's all relative.

**Jack:** Yeah. And, you know, he really wears those jeans extra tight!

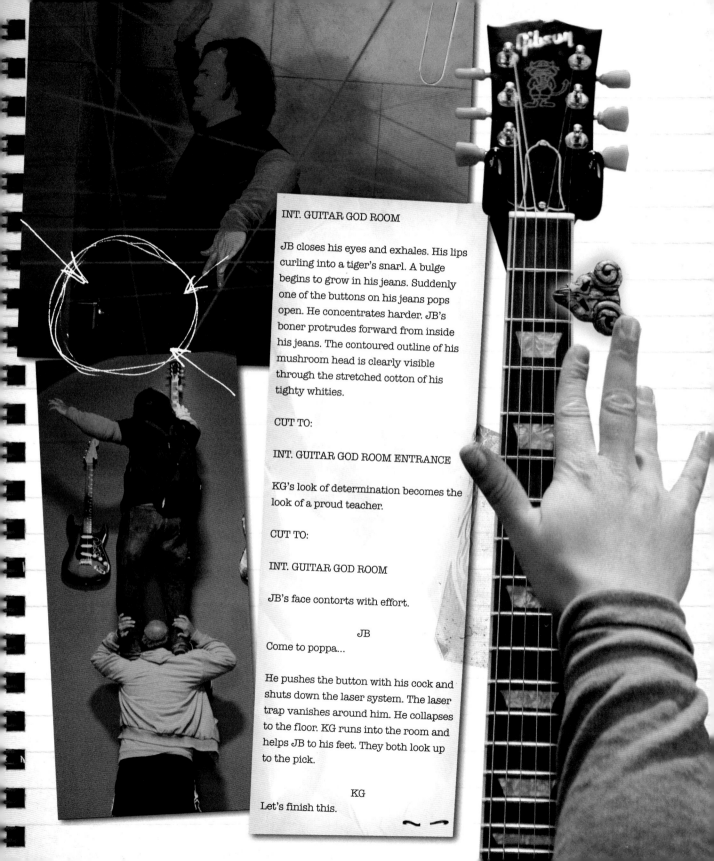

INT. GUITAR GOD ROOM

JB closes his eyes and exhales. His lips curling into a tiger's snarl. A bulge begins to grow in his jeans. Suddenly one of the buttons on his jeans pops open. He concentrates harder. JB's boner protrudes forward from inside his jeans. The contoured outline of his mushroom head is clearly visible through the stretched cotton of his tighty whities.

CUT TO:

INT. GUITAR GOD ROOM ENTRANCE

KG's look of determination becomes the look of a proud teacher.

CUT TO:

INT. GUITAR GOD ROOM

JB's face contorts with effort.

                    JB
Come to poppa...

He pushes the button with his cock and shuts down the laser system. The laser trap vanishes around him. He collapses to the floor. KG runs into the room and helps JB to his feet. They both look up to the pick.

                    KG
Let's finish this.

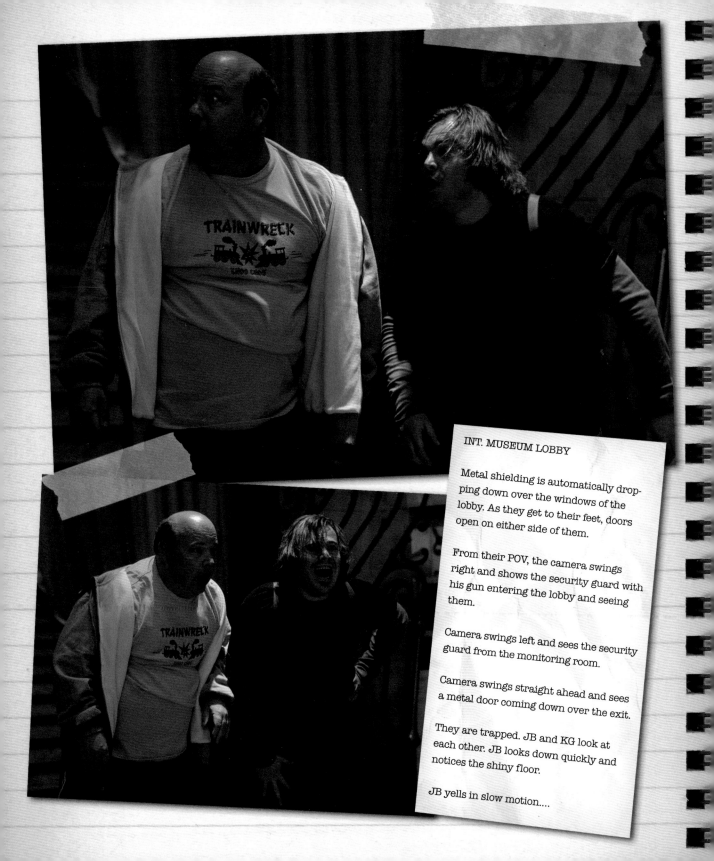

INT. MUSEUM LOBBY

Metal shielding is automatically dropping down over the windows of the lobby. As they get to their feet, doors open on either side of them.

From their POV, the camera swings right and shows the security guard with his gun entering the lobby and seeing them.

Camera swings left and sees the security guard from the monitoring room.

Camera swings straight ahead and sees a metal door coming down over the exit.

They are trapped. JB and KG look at each other. JB looks down quickly and notices the shiny floor.

JB yells in slow motion....

# POWER

**Your escape from the Rock and Roll Museum was pretty epic...**
Kyle: Yeah, we pulled off the most magnificent Power Slide ever witnessed by man.

**How did that feel?**
Jack: It felt good, *reeeaal* good!

**Who are the top power sliders in rock, in your opinion?**
Jack: I'm gonna say Pete Townshend, Jimi Hendrix and Eddie Van Halen.
Kyle: The guy from the Strokes is pretty good. He doesn't power slide, though. He just drops to his knees.
Jack: You know, some of the best power slides are not from good rockers. There are dudes out there — naming no names, they know who they are — who are just good at sliding, not good at rocking.

**What other on stage 'rock moves' do you admire?**
Kyle: I like's Axl's dancing.
Jack: That's a good one. I like that one two times. I also admire Townsend's guitar action, and Ozzy's bat handling.

# SLIDE!"

EXT. ROCK AND ROLL MUSEUM
ENTRANCE – NIGHT

JB and KG run out of the museum.
They stop for a moment to catch their
breath.

                    KG
We made it dude.

                    JB
Totally. Let's get the fuck out of here.

                    KG
Yeah.

OUTSIDE THE ROCK AND ROLL
MUSEUM

Before they can take a step, a voice
stops them in their tracks.

              STRANGER (O.S.)
Nice work boys.

The Stranger from the diner limps out
from the shadows. He is holding a
fifteen inch Bowie knife. JB and KG
stop dead in their tracks.

                 STRANGER
Now toss that pick over here, nice and
slow or I will cut you from hole to hole.

JB and KG are frozen.

                    JB
Then go ahead and kill us man because
there is no way in hell we're giving you
this fucking pick.

                 STRANGER
Okay, so be it. Get over here. I'm going
to fucking stab you!

The Stranger stands in place waiting for them.

The D are boggled.

KG
What?

JB
No. We're not coming over there.

STRANGER
Fine. Just stay where you are then... I'm going to carve your fucking guts out!

He slowly begins to hobble over with his wooden leg. He is slow. He takes his time and is out of breath as he comes towards them.

The D look at each other. The man is clearly not a threat.

KG
Dude, he's really slow.

JB
Yeah. You know why? He's got that wooden leg.

KG
Oh.

The Stranger is still working on making his way to The D.

STRANGER
I'm going to slice out your eyes and your balls... And then I'm going to stick your eyes in your ball-sack and your balls in your eyeholes!

The D continue to watch the man slowly approach.

KG
Dude, we could totally out run him.

JB
Totally. Let's bail.

They turn and jog towards the car. They start it up and drive away. The Stranger attempts to chase after them but can't walk any faster. He finally stops.

STRANGER
Come back here! Come back here with my pick! It belongs to me! It belongs to me!

A bright search light shines onto the Stranger's back. He spins around and is blinded in the beam.

POLICE (O.S.)
Freeze! Drop your weapon!

STRANGER
You'll have to catch me first!

The Stranger turns around slowly. As he begins to take his first step away from the police, they simply walk up behind him and handcuff him.

**TWO KINGS.**

"Now we have the power. We shall carry on its ancient legacy."

You evaded the Stranger with ease, and headed back to Al's Bar. But on the way, due to a misunderstanding over a broken tail light, you got into a car chase — in Lee's car. What was it like filming the movie's big action sequence?

**Jack:** It was fucking dangerous.

**Kyle:** But because of the training I had in Maximum Over Thruster, I was completely prepared for every curve, for every jump. I had to use all of my rocking sauce, but I came through, big time.

**Jack:** It was really scary because we didn't have a stunt driver and Kyle was driving about 127 miles per hour. I was mostly scared for the fucking cameraman who was on the hood of the car. Luckily he was strapped in tight!

**Kyle:** We actually got it in one take, the entire sequence. We had over 37 cameras set up.

INT. LEE'S APARTMENT

Lee is calm and happily sitting down with a Hungry Man Turkey and Gravy TV dinner. He places it on a TV tray with a glass of iced tea. He picks up his remote and turns on the television.

A breaking news story has cut into the normal programming. It's a car chase somewhere in Los Angeles.

He watches as he eats.

              LEE
          (to himself)
Cool. A car chase.

He turns up the volume.

The camera focuses on the television broadcast.

              FEMALE REPORTER (V.O.)
We're coming to you live from the Action News Helicopter. This chase has been going on for the past ten minutes. These fugitives appear to have no interest in surrender wouldn't you say so Larry?

The helicopter camera zooms in on Lee's car. Though extremely damaged, it still looks familiar to him. He slowly puts down his fork and leans forward. He gets a curious look on his face. The car is weaving through traffic as squad cars chase after it.

              MALE REPORTER (V.O.)
Absolutely Linda, the perpetrators are reportedly two white males, heavy set, possibly armed. We don't know at this time if the car is stolen. As you can see the car is severely damaged and police

haven't been able to get a clear ID. We do know it is a blue Cutlass Supreme...

CUT TO:

CLOSE UP - LEE'S FACE

Lee puts down his fork before taking his next bite. He picks up the phone. He begins to dial but then has second thoughts. He feels guilty doubting KG and JB's promise. He mutes the sound on the TV and decides to call just to be sure.

CUT TO:

INT. LEE'S CAR

JB is hanging onto the ceiling as they make a hard turn. Police sirens are blaring. The car phone rings. They look at each other. JB picks up the phone.

JB

Yeah?

INT. LEE'S APARTMENT

Lee is on the phone while watching TV.

LEE

Hey guys. It's Lee. I was just checking
in. Is everything okay?

INT. LEE'S CAR

JB's face is pained upon hearing Lee's
voice.

JB

Yeah buddy, everything's cool. Super
cool.

INT. LEE'S APARTMENT

LEE

Um... So where are you guys?

INT. LEE'S CAR

JB

We're at... the drive-in, man. It's a bitchin'

movie. We're watching... uh... Cop Chase
3. Have you seen it yet? AHH!

INT. LEE'S APARTMENT

As JB screams, Lee watches the car on
television crash through bushes. He can
hear the sound of the snapping
branches over the phone.

LEE

No. I haven't seen that one... It sounds
scary though.

On the television, Lee's car turns to
avoid some police blocking a street. It
goes off the road and down a long stair-
case. JB's voice bounces in sync with
the car going down the stairs.

INT. LEE'S CAR

JB
(bouncing)

Yeah dude, it's really fucking scary. I'm
fucking shaking right now I'm so
scared.

INT. LEE'S APARTMENT

LEE

Wow. So, how did the big meeting go?

The car on television skids and races
down the highway. He hears the skid
through the phone.

CUT TO:

INT. LEE'S CAR

JB
(friendly and terrified)

Awesome! We'll tell you all about it
when we see you. Let me call you back
dude! You're making us miss the movie!

JB hangs up the phone and braces
himself as they drive at top speed.

KG is blurry eyed. His hands tighten on
the steering wheel.

KG
(total Zen)

I can do it.

EXT. AL'S BAR – BACK DOOR

Paul F. Tompkins is standing outside smoking a cigarette.

OPEN MIC HOST
Oh, hey guys. You're running a little late. We got one slot left. You got any new material?

JB
What we got's gonna blow your fucking nuts off pal.

KG
Just dust off the stage and step aside.

OPEN MIC HOST
Oh ho ho. Alright. Well, you're up whenever you're ready, big shots.

Paul F. Tompkins steps inside the doorway. He watches something inside the bar.

JB
Let's rock balls!

JB starts to walk towards the stage door.

KG
Do you still have the pick?

JB holds up the magical pick.

JB
Yeah. I got it. Let's go.

KG
Dude... I think I should use it tonight and you can use it next time.

JB
No, I should use it tonight. I'm the lead singer!

KG
It's a guitar pick! I'm the lead guitarist!

JB

Don't freak out on me man. Let's just work this out rationally. We will take turns with it. I'll use it now and you'll use it later.

KG

I'm not freaking out! You're freaking out. Just let me hold the pick for one fucking second.

JB

You're never gonna touch this fucking pick.

KG tries to grab the pick out of JB's hand. JB pulls away and KG drags him to the ground. They wrestle for the pick. JB yanks on the pick with all his might but KG refuses to let go. It's a tug of war. Suddenly the pick snaps in half.

CUT TO:

CLOSE UP OF TWO HALVES OF THE PICK

Each half of the pick falls to the floor in slow motion. After landing their magical green glow slowly fades away.

CUT TO:

EXT. AL'S BAR – BACK DOOR

JB and KG are standing over the pieces of the pick in horror.

JB AND KG

Noooo!!!

They fall to their knees in despair. They weep.

The door opens.

OPEN MIC HOST

Hey come on you guys, the crowd's getting restless. Hey? What's wrong?

JB tries to speak but it comes out squeaky and childish.

JB
(crying)

We can't go on. We had the Demon's Pick... and we broke it and now our masterpiece won't happen and we can't pay the rent because we won't be fueled by Satan!

He holds up the piece of the pick.

KG is sitting on the ground with his face in his hands. He is crying.

Paul F. Tompkins takes on a motherly manner with them. He kneels down by their sides.

OPEN MIC HOST
You guys really think a satanic guitar pick is going to make you rock better? Guys, Satan isn't in guitar pick. He's inside all of us. He's in here...

He taps JB on the chest over his heart.

OPEN MIC HOST
...in your hearts. He's what makes us not want to go to work in the morning, or exercise, or tell the truth. He's what makes us like to party and have sex with each other all night long. He's that little voice in your mind that says "Fuck you" to people you hate.

The D are touched as they listen. Their eyes widen like hopeful children.

OPEN MIC HOST
Now you two can fight on the ground and cry like babies, or you can go out there like *friends* and rock. Now what's it gonna be?

JB and KG stand up.

KG
Let's go out there and show them what Tenacious D is all about.

JB
Yeah. I've already got a pick anyways.

JB reaches into his pocket and pulls out the pick that KG gave him when they first met. He holds it up revealing KG's handwritten initials.

KG nods to him.

They march through the stage door like brave warriors into battle.

And so we reach the showstopping finale of the movie, which recounts your famous encounter with a certain shiny demon...

**Jack:** Yeah. The D battle Satan, 'Devil Went Down To Georgia' style. We played The Greatest Song In The World, off the top of our fuckin' heads!

**The Greatest Song in the World?**

**Jack:** The *actual* Greatest Song In The World, that we forgot. That we later wrote the tribute to.

**You remembered it then?**

**Jack:** Yes, we remembered it. We had to go to a hypno-therapist. He regressed us back to the time when we originally came up with it.

**Kyle:** We had to do regression therapy.

**Jack:** Yes, a therapist, also an exorcist.

**Kyle:** We actually challenged Satan to a Rock-Off. And the demon code required him to engage...

EXT. AL'S BAR

Once the D have left, Paul F Tompkins makes sure that the coast is clear. He picks up the two halves and starts walking away from the bar. He stops and turns to face camera. His body begins to tremble and spasm as his fists tighten on the shards. He doubles over in pain and soon ignites and grows into the 10 foot Demon. (Seen in the paintings.) It is Satan himself.

CUT TO:

EXT. AL'S BAR

JB and KG walk back out of the bar.

JB
...We better just use it anyway. I'll use half and you'll use half. Who knows maybe it still...

The D stop in their tracks upon seeing the huge Demon standing in the parking lot.

THE D
Ahh! What the fuck?!

Satan is too mesmerized by the pick to even notice the D are standing near him. He opens his palms and the pieces rise up magically.

The two halves of the pick float up to his broken tooth. They fuse like mercury, filling in the Demon's missing fang.

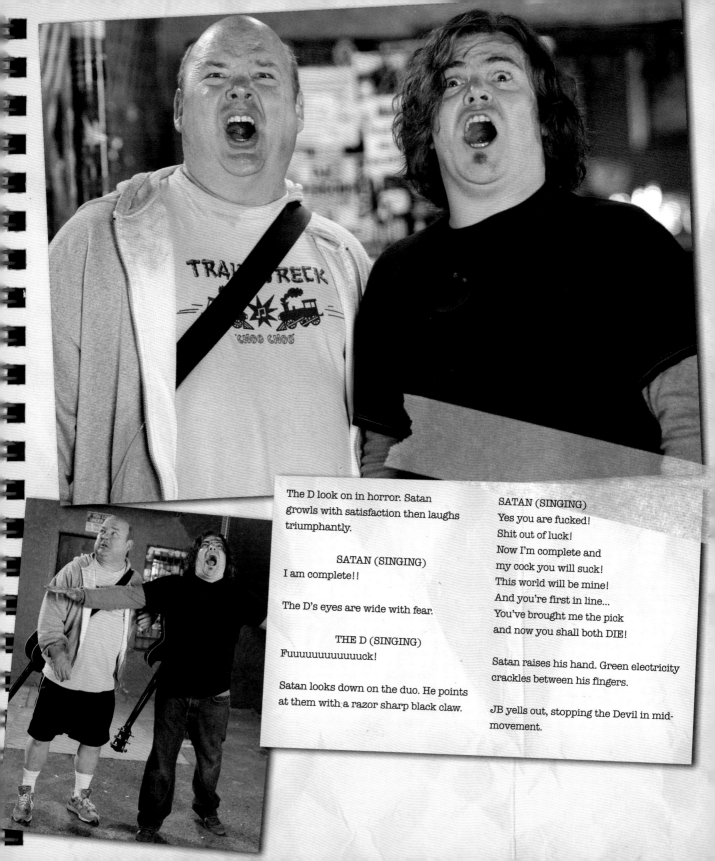

The D look on in horror. Satan growls with satisfaction then laughs triumphantly.

SATAN (SINGING)
I am complete!!

The D's eyes are wide with fear.

THE D (SINGING)
Fuuuuuuuuuuuuuuck!

Satan looks down on the duo. He points at them with a razor sharp black claw.

SATAN (SINGING)
Yes you are fucked!
Shit out of luck!
Now I'm complete and
my cock you will suck!
This world will be mine!
And you're first in line...
You've brought me the pick
and now you shall both DIE!

Satan raises his hand. Green electricity crackles between his fingers.

JB yells out, stopping the Devil in mid-movement.

#### JB (SINGING)
Wait! Wait! Wait! You motherfucker
We challenge you to a Rock-Off
Give us one chance to rock your
socks off...

Satan rolls his eyes. He folds his arms in
annoyance.

#### SATAN
Fuck... FUCK!

He shakes his head in disbelief. He is
holding a burnt ancient scroll. It's his
Demon Contract.

#### SATAN (SINGING)
Fuck... The Demon Code prevents me
from declining a Rock-Off
challenge. What are your terms?
What's the catch?

#### JB (SINGING)
If we win
You must take your sorry ass back to
hell and also you will have to pay our
rent!

KG is overwhelmed and scared. He
looks at JB and then back to Satan in
disbelief.

Satan thinks about JB's offer.

#### SATAN (SINGING)
And what if I win?

#### JB
Then you can take Kage back to hell...

KG eyes open wide. He turns to JB.

#### KG
WHAT?! What the fuck are you talking
about?

#### JB
Trust me Kage, it's the ONLY way.

JB turns back to Satan

#### JB (SINGING)
...To be your little bitch.

Satan is impatient to destroy the world.
He waited too long for this.

#### SATAN
Fine. Let the Rock-Off begin!

I'M THE DEVIL! I LOVE METAL!

CHECK THIS RIFF.
IT'S FUCKING TASTY!

"I'm the Devil I can do what I want!
Whatever I've got I'm gonna' flaunt
There's never been a Rock-Off
that I've ever lost!"

I can't wait to take Kage back to Hell!
I'm gonna' fill him with my hot Demon gel!
I'll make him squeal like my Scarlet Pimpernel!

KG is comatose with dread.

Jack steps in between Satan and Kyle.

JB

NO!

Satan steps back.

The arena of amplifiers disappears with Satan's shock.

JB (TO KG)

Okay, come on Kage. It's masterpiece time. We can do this. We've got shit he doesn't have!

Satan sneers.

Jack jumps with impatience as he speaks. Kyle takes a wild stab at a chord progression.

JB

Yeah! That's what I'm talking about.

JB shows enthusiasm but the song is lame. He searches frantically for lyrics as he is singing them.

JB (SINGING)

Like a cheetah in the night...
Eating rabbits at the speed of light.
And an... Elephant stomp...
And a fucking... Something... Whomp!
It's just the greatest song in the world!
It's the best song that we got
and we like it... Quite a lot...
It's just the greatest song in the world.

Jack drops to his knee and holds up a lighter. Their stage show is only one disposal lighter flame.

Satan is unimpressed. He shakes his head while pinching his fingers between his eyes. He looks up to the sky in disbelief. He's had enough of their lame song.

SATAN

That song was lame! I've had enought of this. Kage, you're coming with me! Taste my lightning, fucker!

Satan raises his hands and a powerful bolt shoots at KG.

In slow motion, JB dives in front of the bolt.

JB

Nooooo!

The bolt strikes JB's guitar but is deflected by the pearl inlay of clouds and lightning. The bolt ricochets back at Satan.

The shot blows off the tip of Satan's horn. His broken horn smokes from the blast.

SATAN
NO! FUCK! You broke my horn! Where is it? No! I'm not complete!!! I'm not complete!!!

The tip of Satan's horn bounces and lands at JB's feet. He quickly picks it up. JB raises his hand and repeats the ancient spell they learned at Guitar Center.

JB
From whence you came
You shall remain
Until you are complete again!

Satan freezes in shock. His eyes open wide. He suddenly is jerked back. He feels a force pulling him.

Several yards behind him, a fiery hole opens in the ground.

He looks back to it in fear.

SATAN

Nooooo!

It's a well to hell. It pulls at Satan and knocks him off his feet. Satan struggles to get at JB and KG but is dragged across the ground towards the hole as if it were a vacuum. He scratches at the ground as he screams. The parking lot pavement is scarred by his long claws.

SATAN

Fuck you Kage! And fuck you Jables! I'll get you Tenacious D!

Satan is pulled into the hole and can be heard falling back to the fires of hell. The ground quickly closes over him. As the smoke clears, JB and KG stand holding the tip of Satan's horn.

They slowly turn to each other and telepathically communicate a mutual respect. They nod. Their friendship is a masterpiece.

They walk off through the alley.

INT. KG'S APARTMENT DAY

The D sit on the couch.

They sit with their guitars. The tape recorder sits in front of them. They are working on a song.

JB (STONEY)
Dude. We fucking beat the Devil! That was such a monster jam. How did that fucking song go that we were playing? That was like, the best song in the world! How'd that thing go?

KG searches on his guitar.

KG
I know... I can't remember.

JB
Fuck.

KG
Whatever dude, let's lay down some new hot tracks right now.

JB
Good call. I know just the thing to get the juices a flowin'. Pass me the B.O.D.

KG
The B.O.D?

JB
The Bong of Destiny?!

KG
Right.

KG reaches out of frame and brings up the broken piece of Satan's horn. It has been converted into a homemade bong. The "Bong of Destiny", if you will.

They each take a huge hit from the horn and hold it in...

JB (HOLDING IN HIT)
Record... Hit record...

KG presses record on the tape recorder.

The D exhale the smoke into camera. The smoke glows green and sparkles with energy. Tis a magical bong indeed.

JB counts off

JB
Two, three, four...

CUT TO BLACK.

# THE END!

## The Pick of Destiny

In Venice Beach there was a man named Kage,
When he was busting he was all the rage.
He met Jables and he taught him well,
All the techniques that were developed in Hell.

Cock push-ups and the power slide,
Gig simulation - now there's nowhere to hide.
They formed a band named Tenacious D,
And then they got the Pick of Destiny.

It was the Pick!
Of Destiny

You know we're rocking cause it's fucking insane

It was the Pick!
Of Destiny

More precious than a diamond or a platinum chain

Cause he who is sleazy, is easy to pleasey,
She who is juicy, must be loosey-goosey,
And he who is groovy, must be in my booty

So come on!

The wizard and the demon had a battle royale,
The demon almost killed him with an evil kapow,
But then he broke his tooth and thus the demon said 'Ow!'

Cause it's the Pick!
Of destiny
You know they be rocking cause it's fucking insane

It was the Pick!
Of Destiny
You know our movie's better than Citizen Kane

Cause he who's a geezer must live in my freezer,
And she who's a diva, must go to Geneva
And he who is groovy, must get in my booty

It's called the Pick of Destiny
The Pick of Destiny

**So, you beat the Devil!**

Jack: Yeah, The D emerge victorious, saving not only ourselves but the whole of humanity!

**Tell us about the final song, over the end credits.**

Kyle: Actually it's kind of a recap of the entire movie.

Jack: It's also a shameless, self-promoting power jam. It's got hit written all over it!

Kyle: To quote Dave Grohl who played drums, right after he knocked it out in one take, 'That song is a big old stinky hit!'

Jack: Yeah. That's what he said.

**You sing that movie is better than** *Citizen Kane*. **That's a bold claim...**

Kyle: *Citizen Kane* has no rock in it! It has no car chase either. And ours is in colour. *Citizen Kane* is only in black and white.

Jack: It also has no money shot! You've gotta have a money shot if you want to fuckin' build a classic!

"THE D EMERGE VICTORIOUS, SAVING NOT ONLY OURSELVES BUT THE WHOLE OF HUMANITY!"

**Where's the money shot in the D movie?**

Jack: Well OK, there's no money shot per se, but when my cock deactivates the lasers that's kinda like I came: Ooooouuuuuurrrgghhh! There are a lot of parts in the movie that will hopefully make an audience feel like they've just had a delicious orgasm!

**Nice! Does the movie have a message though, a moral to be learned?**

Jack: The message of the movie is: Be yourself and the rest will work itself out.

Kyle: Wow.

Jack: Unless you're an asshole.

Kyle: [mad laughter]

Jack: Then be someone else.

Kyle: Never attempt to rock without the proper preparation.

Jack: That's right. Know your song well before you start to sing it.

Kyle: Uh-huh. And just because it looks like you can rock as hard as us...

**Yes?**

Kyle: ...you can't!

Jack: Actually that's the moral. Don't try to be as good as the D.

Time for some final questions. It's obvious that the D are fiercely committed to their craft. Is there anything you wouldn't do for rock?

**Jack:** I would climb the highest mountain and I would sail the seven seas. Kage, is there anything you wouldn't do?

**Kyle:** Anything I wouldn't do...? I wouldn't give up my TiVo.

**Jack:** Wait a second. You're saying you would do anything for rock, but you won't do that?

**Kyle:** [cracks up] Yes! That's what Meat Loaf was singing about! You finally figured it out! [sings] '...but I won't do thaaaaaa-a-a-a-at!'

So you wouldn't give up your TiVo?

**Kyle:** No, but I will do *eee-e-e-e*very-thing else!

JB, what wouldn't you do?

**Jack:** I'm just gonna ride with Kage. It would be hard to beat the TiVo one...

Would you even drop trou, and squeeze out a Cleveland Steamer on someone's chest?

**Jack:** No...Yes! That I would do!

Another key question that needs to be answered: What's your favourite posish?

**Jack:** I'm gonna say, mish! Or, Doctor McDogerty!

What the hell is that?

**Jack:** That's basically a fancy way of saying doggy style. Kyle?

**Kyle:** I like to stand on my head. Or have my girl do the splits... on a balance beam. And enter that way.

**Jack:** Enter Sandmaaaan!

**Well, that about wraps it up. Any final message to your fans?**
**Kyle:** Thanks for buying this book!
**Jack:** The D loves you.

POSSIBLE SEQUEL IDEAS:

# TENACIOUS D

WILL RETURN
IN

YOU, ME, AND THE ~~CRACK WE CREATE~~

# RETURN TO ZANZIBAR!

# 10 Commandments of the D

1. Never stop Rocking.

2. Legalize all drugs.

3. Quit your day job.

4. All Religion should be taxed.

5. Cut down on carbohydrates.

6. Fuck her gently.

7. Never believe what people tell you after a show.

8. Always take a spoon full of Metamucil after a heavy day of eating.

9. Get at least 9 hours of sleep a day.

10. Eatin' ain't cheatin'.

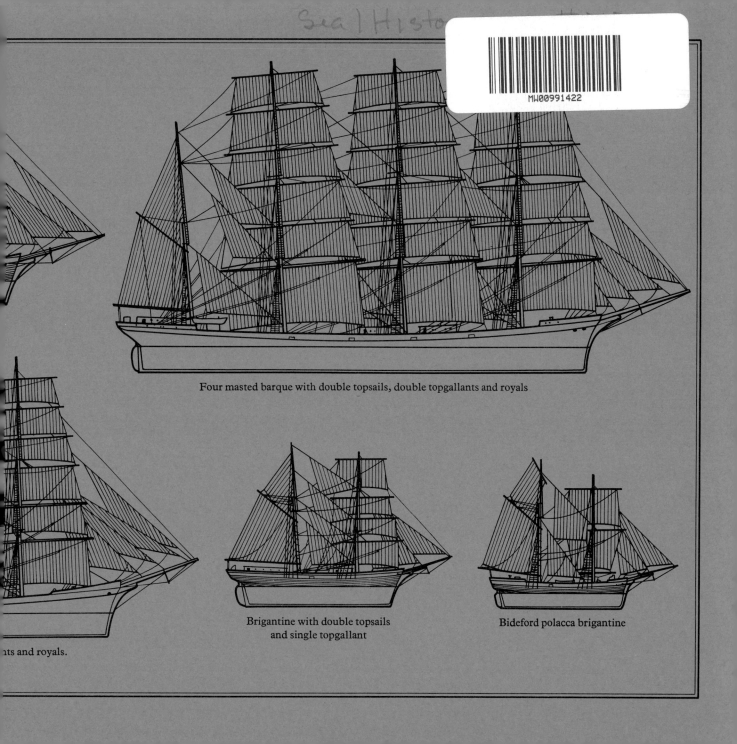

Four masted barque with double topsails, double topgallants and royals

nts and royals.

Brigantine with double topsails
and single topgallant

Bideford polacca brigantine

(front cover) The barque *Peeress*. This vessel was built at Sunderland in 1859 as a full-rigged ship. In 1884 she was converted to barque rig and she is depicted hove-to in this painting in the National Maritime Museum by Richard Henry Nibbs (1816–1893). She was broken up in 1889.

(back cover) This painting by Arthur Briscoe (1873–1943) in the National Maritime Museum is titled 'Clewing up the Main-sail in Heavy Weather'. It illustrates normal working conditions in one of the big iron or steel square-rigged merchant sailing vessels built in the latter part of the 19th century.

© Crown copyright 1980
First published 1980

ISBN 0 11 290317 7

Design by HMSO Graphic Design

Printed in England for
Her Majesty's Stationery Office
by W. S. Cowell Ltd, Ipswich

Dd 696314   K160

National Maritime Museum

# THE SHIP

## The life and death of the Merchant Sailing Ship

### 1815-1965

**Basil Greenhill**

*London*
Her Majesty's Stationery Office

# Contents

Foreword   3

Author's note   4

The Old Ships, 1815–1850   5

The New Ships, 1850–1865   20

The Industrial Revolution goes to sea, 1865–1909   30

Resurrection and the long goodbye, 1915–1965   49

Epilogue   58

Index   60

The *Mary* of Truro, a coasting smack
of a general type which remained in
use in south west England from the
1600s to the 1950s, was built by Hugh
Stephens at Devoran, Nr Truro,
Cornwall in 1875 and after 90 years of
seafaring became derelict at Sharpness,
Gloucestershire in the 1960s

# Foreword

Not many years ago it was almost customary to suggest that the expansion of Britain's world-wide trading empire during the 19th century was based principally on the steady development of the commercial steamship. British predominance, it was assumed, was largely the consequence of cheap and abundant coal, the efficiency of the iron industry and the skill and inventiveness of British engineers. Some historians described the second half of the century as 'The Age of Iron and Steel', thus contributing to the myth that steamships 'made the British Empire possible'.

Actually, as Basil Greenhill makes clear in the final volume in this series to be concerned with the history of the sailing ship, the great, and even glorious, days of sail came not before, but after mid-century; the transition to the iron and steel cargo steamer was not completed until the late 1890s. During a score and more years after 1850, the square-rigged wooden (and subsequently iron) merchant vessel achieved its highest efficiency as a long-distance carrier. Although the steamer had wedged its way into the overseas trade, chiefly as a mail and passenger carrier, the evolving sailing ship – faster than her predecessors, with double the space for cargo in proportion to tonnage, and manned by about one third the number of crew hitherto required – dominated the ocean trades. Even when the opening of the Suez Canal in 1869 reduced the longest gap between coaling stations from some 5000 to 2000 miles, most of the traffic to the Bay of Bengal, the East Indies, South America or Australia, was still conducted by the sailing ship – the economic carrier of such bulky commodities as iron and coal, the jute and rice of India and Burma, the wool of Australia, the nitrate fertilizer of Chile and the wheat of California.

The proportionately higher cargo capacity of the sailer offering proportionately lower freight rates than were possible for the machine-driven vessel, served to confirm an ascendancy in ocean commerce until the coming of the perfected high pressure marine engine. Not until the 80s, with the help of steel boiler plates and tubes, did the triple-expansion engine sound the death knell of the sailing ship. In 1881, the SS *Aberdeen*, fitted with triple expansion engines, was launched from Napier's yard in Glasgow. She reached Melbourne within 42 days under a steam pressure of 125 lbs. By the end of 1884, with the improvement of boilers, the 150 mark had been reached. In 1887 the 150 pressure mark was passed, and shortly after, the 200 – a pressure per square inch requiring only a fraction more than a pound of coal per horse-power per hour. The original low pressure engine had often required more than ten. The final stage in the gradual annihilation of sail had at long last been reached.

There was, indeed, a short-lived resurrection following the World War of 1914-18, but few square-riggers survived the post-war depression. Nova Scotian and Danish schooners still plied the North Atlantic carrying salt cod; occasionally, wooden three-masted schooners and ketches were built in Denmark. But during the 40s, they slowly succumbed in the face of rising labour costs and the rapidly increased price of sails and rigging. By the end of the 60s, these heirs of giant fleets had passed away.

3

# Author's note

It is good and proper that the Director of the National Maritime Museum, author of the definitive work on British schooners and a distinguished authority on the merchant sailing ship, should have undertaken the task of describing graphically and with skilled care a portentous epoch in the history of ocean transport, when the sailing ship, after reaching new heights of efficiency and even beauty, surrendered her world mastery to the machine.

Gerald S. Graham
RHODES PROFESSOR OF IMPERIAL HISTORY
London University, 1949–70

This engraving shows a two-masted schooner of the second half of the 19th century. The engraving was used as a letter heading by John Stephens of Par and Fowey in Cornwall who managed a fleet of these vessels, employed principally in the trade with salt fish from Newfoundland to European ports. Photo: Basil Greenhill collection

I am greatly indebted to Professor Gerald Graham for much help and advice and indeed for inspiring this study through his own pioneering paper 'The Ascendancy of the Sailing Ship, 1850–85', read in synopsis at the International Congress of Historical Sciences in Rome in September 1955 and published in the *Economic History Review*, Volume IX, No. 1. I also wish to express my debt to Captain W.J.Lewis Parker, USCG (retd.), whose comment on an early draft was most constructive, to Captain Karl Kåhre, Director of the Ålands Sjöfartsmuseum, to William A.Baker of the Francis Russell Hart Nautical Museum at the Massachusetts Institute of Technology, and to Robin Craig.

I hope that the publication of the relevant volumes in this series will point the way to filling a large and vitally important gap in the economic history of Britain. It is time there was a full scale study of merchant shipping of the years between the Battle of Waterloo and the Second World War. The source material is massive, accessible, and with modern techniques relatively easy to handle. The subject touches upon all aspects of life in this country at a time when it was developing into the first modern state and the industry was vitally important to that development. It should receive proper attention.

Basil Greenhill
DIRECTOR, NATIONAL MARITIME MUSEUM

# The Old Ships, 1815-1850

This short book is about the merchant sailing vessel in Europe (and mainly northern Europe at that) and North America, with no more than odd references to vessels of European type built elsewhere in the world. The story of the merchant shipping industries of these two continents, which were overwhelmingly more important in the period covered than those of the rest of the world put together, is almost too complex to condense into the space available. To discuss in addition the indigenous seaborne traffics of China, the Bay of Bengal, the Arabian Sea and the coasts of South America in the 19th century, interesting though they are, is not possible.

After centuries of active life, culminating in revolutionary increases in efficiency, size and numbers, the terminal sickness of the merchant sailing vessel in the western world occupied only the years from 1885 to 1909. The death was followed by a brief but indisputable resurrection which lasted from 1916 until the early 1920s and by a long goodbye persisting for small vessels, thanks to the diesel engine, into the 1960s.

It has been a much misunderstood demise. Often, indeed usually, the history has been represented as one of a gradual process with the merchant sailing vessel under continuous threat and consequent slow attrition throughout the 19th century. It has been said many times that the sailing vessel was doomed as soon as the first steam vessel paddled her way along a canal. In fact the sailing vessel was under no threat at all until the development to commercial success of the compound-engined steamship in 1865 and not doomed until the widespread adoption of

triple expansion engines between 1881 and 1885. Even then thousands of British sailing vessels continued to carry cargoes all over the world and the owners of sailing tonnage in Britain exploited the boom years of the late 1880s and early 1890s to the extent that over 250 large steel square-rigged vessels were built at that time. On the East and West coasts of the United States more than 220 four-masted schooners and big barquentines were launched over the same years.

It has been asserted that sailing vessels reached the culmination of their development in the tea trade to Britain from China. This conception is equally unreal. The tea clipper was really a relatively unimportant side-line in the long history of the merchant sailing ship. Looking back into history, when the specific demand for fast vessels occurs, they appear, either for some kind of special cargo carrying purpose, or for special purposes, such as blockade running, smuggling, intercepting other fast vessels, carrying dispatches, or struggling to maintain a fast and regular 'packet', that is, parcel and passenger delivery service, around the coasts of Europe in competition with stage coaches, or across the North Atlantic when the demand was such that very high fares and charges could be levied. But at all times the very fast sailing vessel represented only a small part of the total of contemporary merchant shipping activity and had relatively little influence on the industry as a whole.

The story of the life and death of the merchant sailing ship can only be properly appreciated as part of a very much wider scene, that is, the industrial history of the 19th century, with all that that implies

Plate 1 (left) The barque *Countess of Bective,* seen on the right, built in 1843, and the full-rigged ship *Mary Dugdale,* built at Hull in 1835, both typical of their period, with their deep narrow hulls, photographed in Swansea in 1844 or '45. The *Dugdale's* fore and main topsail yards and all her topgallant and royal yards with their rigging have been sent down on deck and her fore top-gallant mast is housed on the fore side of the topmast.
Photo: National Maritime Museum

Plate 2 (right) The brig *Mary* of St Ives and the schooner *Liberty* of Teign-mouth, the latter built in 1823, lying on the mud off Swansea Harbour at low tide in 1844 or '45. The *Mary* has stern windows, illuminating her great cabin. The *Liberty* has the short fore topsail and topgallant yards associated with 18th-century schooners.
Photo: National Maritime Museum

in terms of political, financial and colonial develop-ment. Treated from only a relatively slightly different angle the subject might equally well and properly be entitled 'The Rise of the Steam Tramp', for the decline of sail is inextricably intertwined with the rise of the steam tramp after 1865. It is one of the paradoxes of industrial history that the merchant sailing vessel was a machine which in the late 19th century was developed out of all recognition in terms of efficiency and capability when it was clearly obsolete.

The circumstances of the death of the merchant sailing vessel and what followed can only be pre-sented, explained and understood against the back-ground of the long centuries of healthy life which had preceded it and which have been described in the earlier volumes of this series on the history of the ship. In the 1820s, 30s and 40s the merchant sailing

vessel enjoyed the generally expanding prosperity of industry as a whole and in her old slow way she was very much alive. Imagine, then, a tidal harbour; Swansea will do since we happen to have an excellent series of photographs of the port in the early 1840s. The ships there represent very well the ordinary merchant vessels of the period. They are wooden full-rigged ships, barques and brigs, none of them over 500 tons register under the current method of measuring tons (Plate 1). Such vessels might be found anywhere at that time. But, in addition, Swansea in the early 1840s had schooners as regular visitors (Plate 2). These were the years when the schooner was beginning to come into general use in Britain. The rig, in which gaff and boom sails pro-vided the main area of canvas, was of European origin, but it had been developed in eastern North America in the 18th century. Needing less capital to

construct, fewer men to sail and being less expensive to maintain than the small brigs and the big smacks which had been the normal small merchant vessels of the early 19th century, by the 1840s schooners were becoming fairly common, especially in ports with a North American trade.

The harbour at Swansea dried out on each tide, so twice a day the vessels had to sit on the mud, as they are shown in Plate 1. This meant that they had to be flat floored, box sectioned, amidships and for a number of frames fore and aft of amidships, so that they could sit upright. Most British harbours were still without floating docks, so most vessels had to deal with this situation from time to time. There were many other factors which made for fullness of hull form and complexity and weakness in rigging. Except in a few businesses, there were almost no forces in play to make profitable any degree of development, so these ships were little changed from the merchant sailing vessels of the previous century. Flax canvas was still relatively loosely woven and made baggy sails which stretched and changed shape, particularly when wet. Machine manufactured tight woven cotton canvas was still some years away, as was readily available iron wire for standing rigging, so natural fibre rope was still used entirely. To be strong enough this rope had to be very bulky and it required endless attention, setting it up against stretch, protecting it from wear and the effects of weather. Masts, yards, gaffs and booms were all made of wood because industry had not reached the stage at which it could provide cheap shaped iron tubular spars. The wood, like the wood of which the hull was entirely constructed, except for some fastenings and possibly some iron knees and straps, split, rotted, broke and wore away. The whole vessel was really an organic structure. And it was a flexible structure built up of thousands of small pieces of timber secured together with fastenings, iron pins and

wooden pins, and the iron pins and the iron fittings on deck and on the masts and in the rigging cost a not inconsiderable fraction of the total cost of construction of the vessel.

The wooden sailing vessel required the same sort of endless attention as a herd of cows or a team of oxen or draught horses. She had to be pumped regularly, after a few years of working life pumped usually several times a day when laden at sea, for she leaked continuously through the hundreds of joints in her outer skin and through the seams between her planks. The caulking, that is the sealing, comprising oakum driven in hard between the planks and sealed with pitch had to be examined, repaired and renewed regularly. The fresh water from the rain had to be kept out of her, and in particular fresh water had to be discouraged from leaking down the heads of the frames, where it would rapidly do terrible damage through the rot which followed. At the same time the decks could not be left to get dry. If they were not washed down with salt water at least once, and in a hot climate several times, a day, then the deck planking would dry out, shrink, and the caulking between the planks would become loose and the seams leak, and quite apart from the discomfort to the crew below deck and the damage to the cargo, once again increased and accelerating rot would follow.

All the ropes in the running rigging had to be tended, their ends had to be kept from fraying out, they had to be turned end to end periodically to balance the wear on them, splices – joins in the ropes made narrow enough to go through the blocks – had to be renewed, whole ropes had to be replaced. Blocks had to be oiled, that is, the timber cases conserved with linseed and examined for cracks and other damage. Spars had to be watched for shakes and for rot and where the complex rigging ironwork, spider bands, cranes, boom irons, was joined to them they were particularly vulnerable. The ironwork itself had to be chipped and painted, and in particular the bolts which held it to the spars had to be watched for corrosion and for rot in the adjoining wood, for loose ironwork in the rigging could lead rapidly to a vessel's dismasting. A small barque had about 350 blocks and several miles of rope in her rigging, and perhaps nearly a mile and a half of caulking of oakum and pitch driven into her seams. All this maintenance meant that the masts and spars were frequently sent down on deck, whole sections of masts unrigged for maintenance work in harbour by the vessels' own crews, as can be seen in Plate 1. And this was still the era at sea when a recognised way of dealing with the problem of the windage of the complex spider's web of rigging and spars aloft was partly to unrig the ship in heavy weather. So the immensely complex, heavy and dangerous work of sending down yards and parts of the masts was done, as a matter of course, in a gale at sea with the small vessel throwing herself all over the place and with rain, sleet, or snow into the bargain.

It follows that the men who handled these ships were very highly skilled indeed in their trades. Each vessel was still largely a self-supporting entity in her voyaging about the seas of the world. The ships were the heirs to the 'space capsule of the Renaissance', as the first three-masted sailing ships which opened up the world in the late 15th and early 16th centuries have been called. The vessels carried their own livestock, a man in the crew could do the necessary forge work to repair damaged iron fittings, experienced seamen could make sails (Plate 3) and certainly all mature seamen could handle any of the necessary maintenance work in the rigging or on the hull of the vessel. When a vessel lost her bowsprit, for example, she did not limp into the nearest shipyard for repair. The crew made up, from spare timber carried for the purpose, a new spar under the direction of the

carpenter, cleared away the damaged rigging and fitted the new spar into position, however heavy and bulky it was and in any reasonable conditions of wind and sea, and repaired and replaced the damaged rigging as necessary, using material carried on board for just such contingencies.

The methods of navigation used were still rudimentary. Until the middle of the century there were no formal qualifications required of masters and

Plate 3 The square-rigged vessels in the first two plates had the deep single topsails used in all vessels until the early 1860s. Their sails when set looked like these, drying on the American whaling barque *Massachusetts*, built in 1836, photographed in New Bedford Harbour in 1870.
Photo: Mystic Seaport

mates. Examination of contemporary accounts of trans-Atlantic passages in ordinary merchant ships in the 1840s shows that successful and profitable vessels were still being navigated purely by latitude sailing, with no attempt to calculate longitude, as if the nautical almanac and the chronometer, products of the 1760s, had still not existed.

Throughout human history, people who took to the sea in Britain, on the Continent or in North America, did so usually because there was no other way of life open to them. Once caught, the individuals, their families and social groups, the very communities from which they came, became more and more isolated, more cut off from the normal society of the land and of landward looking communities. The very intensity of their occupational specialisation emphasised the social isolation of their calling. And between them and the landsmen, as always, there was a kind of alienation. They even spoke a form of the language which was different from that of the landsman and they were hard to understand. The landsman was suspicious, often frightened of the seaman's alien world, and hid his fear and ignorance in expressed contempt. The seamen met the situation to a degree by retreating into the compensating fantasy of the jolly sailor, conforming to a stereotype which the bulk of society expected of him.

Crew costs were always important. The smaller vessels, the brigs and little barques, much less the schooners, which carried on ocean trade and earned a living for themselves, their crews, masters and shareholders, and part of a living for those who supplied the materials to maintain them and the provisions to outfit them, in the 1830s and 40s often carried crews which would be considered insufficient for an ocean racing yacht today. To take one documented instance, the barque *Civility* of Bideford, 247 tons register, 94.6 feet long, sailed back and forth across the North Atlantic right through the 40s and early 50s with a crew of ten all told. In 1848 four of them, the master, the two mates, and the cook were all from the same family, the Bales who had migrated in 1816 from the agricultural community of Alphington to the nearby seafaring community of Appledore in North Devon and become seamen. In the *Civility* the crew not only sailed the ship, they maintained her at sea and in port and they carried hundreds of emigrants westwards in complete safety to Quebec from Bristol, Plymouth and Bideford and they brought back hundreds of tons of 16 inch squared lumber from the St Lawrence to Britain.

Richard Bale, the Master, was probably less sophisticated than his American counterpart from Boston, or somewhere down east on the Maine coast, sailing with his wife and family on board. But it was in vessels like the *Civility*, and not in the packet ships from Liverpool, that a great many of the $7\frac{1}{2}$ million British and Irish emigrants travelled to North America between 1800 and 1875 to lay the foundations of the modern United States and Canada.

This was not a world into which innovation would readily come unless there were very strong forces at work to make it clearly worthwhile. Those forces were already coming into existence in the 1840s and great changes were imminent, but as yet they had had little effect. The age of reform was going soon to revolutionise merchant shipping as much of the life of industry ashore was to be revolutionised. But in the early 1840s the majority of vessels had been and were still built under the influence of the old tonnage law. This had been introduced in an Act of Parliament of 1773 and when the registration of all merchant vessels became compulsory in 1786, the 1773 tonnage rules were applied to all ships under the new Act to provide for an entry in the Register which was intended to represent the total cargo capacity of the vessel. This legislation remained in force until 1836

Plate 4  The deep narrow hull encouraged by the tonnage measurement rules and the shipbuilding traditions of the early 19th century is well illustrated in this photograph of the barque *Mary Ann Peters*, built at Richibucto in New Brunswick, Canada, in 1835. She has grounded while leaving Bristol City Docks in 1857, bound for West Africa. Shore riggers have helped the crew to send down all her upper masts, spars and rigging, so that the lines rigged from her lower masts to the shore can hold her against falling over on her side and filling on the next flood tide. She was saved to be lost off Bermuda in 1863.
Photo: National Maritime Museum

and for various reasons its effects lingered on and the general type of vessel which was constructed under the influence of the old tonnage law continued to be built widely. Indeed they continued to be built to some extent even after a new Act in 1854 changed the whole picture.

Under the Act of 1773, the tonnage of a vessel was taken to be the result of multiplying her length on deck (from foreside the stem to the afterside of the stern post) minus three-fifths of her maximum breadth (the result of this deduction was supposed to give her keel length) by the maximum breadth and then again by half the maximum breadth (which was supposed to represent the depth of the vessel's hold) and dividing the result by the apparently arbitrary (but possibly traditional) figure of 94. The result was a figure which bore little relation to the actual capacity of the vessel or indeed to her total volume, but one which could easily be obtained, because the measurements could be taken and the calculations made by people with the minimum of formal education. Tonnage by this measurement did give a general indication of the length and breadth of the vessel, but not, of course, of her depth, which was not measured or taken into account in any way.

The result of the application of this formula, into which the depth of the vessel did not enter, to the calculations on which charges for pilotage, light dues, port dues, etc., were based, was to give commercial advantage to deep, narrow, vessels. Consequently British and American shipbuilding traditions (for the United States had introduced similar legislation in 1789) became centred on the deep, narrow vessel with an almost vertical stern post to take maximum advantage in terms of capacity of the arbitrary rating of the keel length as the length on deck less three-fifths of the breadth. The type is beautifully illustrated in Plate 4. The *Mary Ann Peters* because of her great depth, had a splendid capacity for cargo in

relation to her length and breadth, and therefore in relation to the tonnage-based dues which she paid, and this capacity was enhanced by very full bows and the carrying fore and aft of the full midships section which enabled her to sit almost upright on the mud – otherwise she would have turned over in her predicament. Her main disadvantage was that she needed a gale of wind operating on a big area of sail to drive her along and since she lacked the stability and sail-carrying power of a beamier vessel her sails had to be smartly handled. But perhaps the necessity for smart handling was largely irrelevant when the gain in freight on the extra cargo was greater than the cost of the additional rigging and crew, and, if she was in the North American lumber trade, for example (and vessels in this business represented one seventh of the whole British carrying trade in 1820), a vessel could do well if she could comfortably complete her two round voyages to Quebec between March and December each year. She did not look very handsome, though the assessment of the appearance of ships is a very subjective business. On the whole the combined working of the tonnage measurement rules and economic circumstance produced an adequate but unnecessarily unhandy vessel.

The traditions of building represented by the vessels in Plates 1, 2 and 4, were much reinforced by the long Napoleonic Wars, when any advantage of speed was eliminated by the convoy system and all the advantage was with cargo capacity. The deep, narrow ship became firmly established on both sides of the Atlantic, and for all the liberating effects of the alterations in rules for tonnage measurement in the later Merchant Shipping Acts, which no longer put a premium on depth, this type of vessel, later somewhat shallower and beamier and somewhat sharper in hull shape fore and aft, became the normal in the British and American merchant shipping industries into the 1860s.

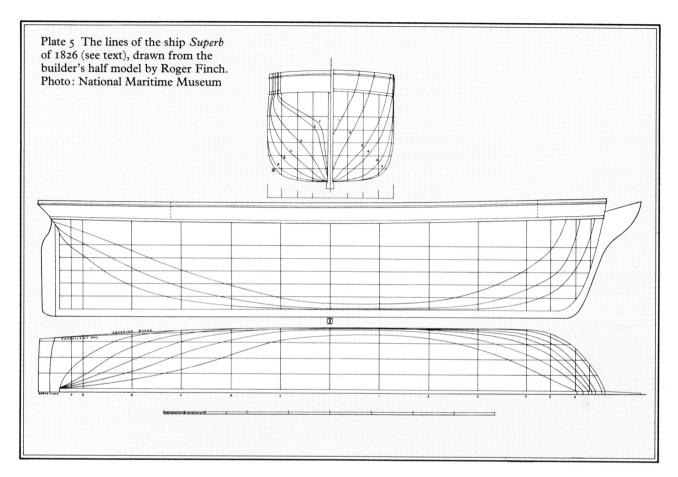

Plate 5 The lines of the ship *Superb*
of 1826 (see text), drawn from the
builder's half model by Roger Finch.
Photo: National Maritime Museum

The drawing in Plate 5 shows the shape of these vessels very well. The lines were taken off a half model of a vessel built at New Bideford, Prince Edward Island, Canada, by William Ellis, a master shipwright who was trained in the naval dockyard at Devonport. After working for Richard Chapman, a very well established shipbuilder at Northam in North Devon, he emigrated at the age of 44 in 1818 to Prince Edward Island where he set up a shipyard on behalf of Thomas Burnard, at the time the leading merchant of Bideford, the next parish to Northam. William Ellis represented the solid traditions of British merchant shipbuilding at this period.

The half model does not match exactly the registered dimensions of any of the numerous vessels built under William Ellis' supervision, but it approximates most closely to those of the *Superb*, launched at New Bideford in 1826 for Thomas Burnard's widow. The *Superb* was a little shorter than this half model to scale, though of approximately the same beam. Given that it is usual to have difficulty in checking model and ship and that it was common practice to add or take out a frame or two and change the rakes of stem and sternpost during construction it is highly likely this model is the *Superb* and was preserved because she was the biggest vessel William Ellis ever built.

The model clearly illustrates the characteristics of the merchant vessels of the period as I have already described them. She also underlines the small size of the normal merchant ship of the 1820s and 30s. The *Superb* was about 130 feet long on deck with a dead-weight tonnage, that is a cargo-carrying capacity, of about 900 tons, but she was one of the only 18 vessels

Plate 6 The schooner rigged bully boat, or skiff, *Clara*, an open boat about 36 feet long of a type still in use on the coasts of Newfoundland in the first half of the 20th century. Photo: Public Archives of Newfoundland

registered as of the port of Bristol in the first four decades of the 19th century which were of 500 tons register or more. The size of the average merchant ship gently increased in the next 20 years, but in the 1840s the *Superb* (which by then had been sold to owners abroad) would still have been an above average size ordinary merchant ship.

There were good reasons for small size. The amount of cargo usually available to be loaded at one time was by modern standards minute. Port facilities were rudimentary and all cargo was hand-worked. Even small vessels took a great time loading and discharging. Many harbours were shallow and simply could not take big vessels, even if the normal conduct of business had stimulated any demand for them or any opportunity to use them with their attendant economies of scale.

Indeed the larger vessels shown in the photographs of Swansea reproduced here represent the ordinary deep sea ships of the 1840s. In the period covered by this chapter thousands of much smaller brigs, brigantines, schooners and smacks, made long sea voyages, to the Baltic, the Mediterranean, the Azores, the West Indies, North America, the Pacific and the Indian Ocean. Long ocean voyages in vessels only 50 or 60 feet long were not uncommon, absurd and uneconomic though the amounts of cargo they could carry seem today.

In the home trade, that is, within the sea limits between the Elbe and Brest, during the Napoleonic Wars the sphere of operation of the Home Fleet and later enshrined in successive Merchant Shipping Acts, the normal vessel was the small brig, brigantine or smack, with a steadily increasing number of schooners, while coastal passages in open boats loaded with cargo were still made in both European and North American waters even in the late 19th century (Plate 6). The small merchant ships which carried coal in vast quantities to London from the

Plate 7  Coasting smacks discharging coal over shutes into
carts on the beach at Porth Gaverne in North Cornwall.
Three horses were needed to pull the laden carts up the
steep roads that lead from the beach. The vessel in the
middle is the *Telegraph* built at Porth Gaverne in 1859.
Photo: Gillis Collection

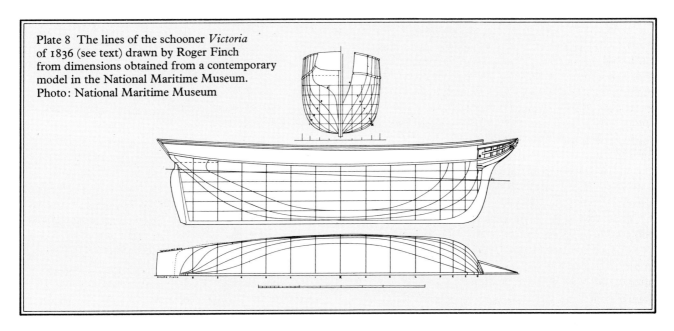

Plate 8  The lines of the schooner *Victoria*
of 1836 (see text) drawn by Roger Finch
from dimensions obtained from a contemporary
model in the National Maritime Museum.
Photo: National Maritime Museum

North East coast and increasingly from there and
from the west coast to other areas where industry
and population were developing were most often
rigged as brigs. As Robin Craig has explained in the
fifth volume in this series, this was a trade peculiarly
susceptible to early penetration by steam vessels and
the classic north east coast collier brig was to vanish
well before the end of the century. Small sailing
vessels carried stone, bricks, grain, household
furniture, groceries, machinery, great quantities of
minerals, cattle, vegetables, salt, glassware, pottery,
china clay, fertiliser, almost everything that needed
to be carried for a developing society as yet badly
served by railways. Where there was no harbour they
went up on the open beach at high tide and discharged into carts before the next flood tide came to
float them off again. Many of the beaches of Britain
were regular places of trade right down into the 20th
century (Plate 7), for the factors which made for the

use of small vessels in the 1820s and 30s together
with the diesel engine were to prolong the small
sailing vessels' life in trade to small ports.

The lines of the schooner *Victoria*, built in Looe
in East Cornwall in 1836, taken from a contemporary
model and reproduced here in Plate 8, show very
well that the influence of the tonnage rules bore on
small vessels no less than on large. She is long,
narrow and deep for her size and like the bigger
square-rigged vessels needed a great press of canvas
to drive her along.

In the 1830s and 40s only the bigger vessels
chartered by the East India Company were larger
than the *Superb* and the other big vessels out of
Bristol. The optimum size of a big merchant ship
was then 600 tons register, perhaps carrying 1000 to
1200 tons of cargo. The bigger East Indiaman were
of 1200 tons to 1400 tons or so register. They remained the largest wooden sailing ships afloat until

the 1850s. They operated in a special and protected trade in which the economies of scale could be exploited, lying in deep water at either end of each passage, assured of big cargoes in each direction, making only one long voyage in each year. They were semi-official vessels serving the growing Indian trade and carrying the growing number of passengers, soldiers, administrators, businessmen with their families who made their lives, or part of them, in India. They carried them out on first appointment and they carried the survivors back on rare home leave.

Of the 18 biggest vessels of the Port of Bristol referred to on page 14, ten were built in Bristol and five in what is now Canada. Dr McGowan in his two volumes in this series draws attention to the importance of the New England colonies as a source of tonnage for the British market in the 17th and 18th centuries. Following the punitive duties on Baltic timber in 1812 and the consequent establishment of a massive Canadian timber trade into Britain, the already well-established Quebec shipbuilding industry expanded and shipbuilding rapidly developed in New Brunswick, Nova Scotia, and Prince Edward Island, financed, initially, from Britain and manned by emigrant craftsmen from this country. This Canadian shipbuilding industry was to play a part, sometimes important, in British merchant shipping history until the end of the 1860s. For instance, in 1840, a boom year, while 1406 vessels were built and registered in Great Britain, totalling 217 000 tons gross, 556 vessels were built in Canada, totalling 122 000 tons gross and many of them were sold to British owners, making a contribution of more than one third of the new tonnage. The vessels were built on speculation more cheaply than was possible in Britain and were of great value to British shipowners in times of boom when British-built tonnage was not available at reasonable prices. Built of softwood, the vessels had a greater cargo capacity than hardwood British vessels and they tended to be faster, when speed mattered.

For the first fifty years of her life (taking the year of the Battle of Waterloo (1815) perhaps as a convenient date of effective birth), the steamship presented no real general commercial threat to the sailing vessel. The long, deep, narrow ships of the 20s, 30s and 40s, with their tall rigs, did not have to compete commercially with steam-driven vessels. The steamer provided entirely new services on short range, high density, passenger routes, she assisted the sailing vessel as a tug, and as a subsidised mail and passenger carrier on the Atlantic and eastern routes she provided a service which did not exist before. In the 1820s nearby parts of the Continent and Ireland were served by paddle-steamers. In the 1830s paddle-steamers had reached Egypt in regular service and after 1835 they provided a service to India via the Isthmus of Suez. All these services were in one way or another subsidised, usually by mail contracts, as was the trans-Atlantic service of the early 1840s. The globe was not circumnavigated by a steam vessel until the mid-1840s. The British naval sloop *Driver* took five years to achieve this feat and for many years afterwards she remained the only steam vessel to have been round the world. The steamship simply could not compete with the mass of sailing vessels which carried the growing trade of the world and it was not capable of competing until three technical and industrial problems had been solved.

The first of these problems was the provision of a more efficient means of propulsion than the paddle. This problem was slowly solved by the introduction of various types of screw propeller which were evolved from the late 1830s.

But the screw propeller was driven through a shaft which, because the machinery in early steam vessels was carried at the point of maximum buoyancy amidships, ran nearly half the length of the vessel. Wooden ships were always flexible structures, built up of thousands of small pieces of timber secured together with fastenings. As should be expected of such structures, they could and did leak continuously after a few years of working life, unless they were built to a standard which made them scarcely economic as cargo carriers. Add to these natural characteristics the vibration of a primitive steam engine and the stresses and strains produced by the torque imposed by the transmission of any reasonable amount of power through the long shaft and the consequence was that the working life of a screw-driven wooden hull was liable to be expensive, short and troublesome.

The successful steam vessel had to be not only screw-driven, but also built of iron. The second requirement, therefore, was for cheap iron to be available in the quantities, sizes and qualities required to build ships of tonnage large enough to carry enough fuel to make ocean voyages. Such iron materials did not become available until the 1840s. The *Great Britain* of 1843, now preserved in Bristol, was in due course to prove to be the first commercially successful large iron screw steamship, though her commercial success was in an operating pattern in which she used her sails alone for longer periods than she steamed. In construction she pointed to the main line of development which steamships were in due course going to follow, just as she showed the practicality of iron wire standing rigging, of a sharp hull which anticipated the big American clipper ships of the 50s by a decade, and of the schooner rig for big ships – to be adopted and developed in North America forty years later.

The iron screw steamship, assisted in varying degrees by sails, had a wider range of operation and was less uneconomic than any of her predecessors.

The use of steam was extended, but still very largely on subsidised routes, or on bulk cargo, luxury cargo, or passenger short haul routes. There the development of the steamer stopped, because the third requirement was still not met – the steam engine was still an uneconomical luxury.

The problem was not simply a matter of fuel costs. The simple steam engines of the 1840s and 50s needed so much coal to fire their boilers that there was literally not enough space left on board to carry a paying cargo on an ocean voyage. So although in the early 1850s big screw-driven iron steamships could be built, they still could not compete with sailing vessels in the general tonnage market, because they had to carry too much fuel to leave room for a cargo big enough to earn a freight which made the vessel profitable to operate. In consequence, as late as the year 1860 wooden sailing vessels, perhaps the bulk of them showing in their design the influence of the old tonnage rules, still made up by far the greater part of the world's merchant shipping tonnage. Indeed in 1860, the total sailing ship gross tonnage (it was not until the Merchant Shipping Act of 1867 that the distinction between net and gross tonnage was introduced for sailing vessels) the greater part of it wooden, registered at United Kingdom ports was 4 204 000. Steam net tonnage, much of it iron, totalled 454 000. It was to be more than two decades after the photographs which illustrate this chapter were taken in Swansea in the early 1840s before the sailing vessel was to feel commercial competition from steamships to any noticeable degree.

But these British sailing vessels did face competition from another source. The end of the revolution in which the United States gained their independence found the new nation with few merchant vessels available. The growth of trade was slow and there were at first few communities in a position to finance the building of vessels of any substantial size, even by the standards of the times. It was in these circumstances that the national preference for the schooner rig, with its low building, operating and manning costs, was confirmed and two-masted schooners became the most numerous of American vessels. Meanwhile larger square-rigged vessels of up to 500 tons were very profitably employed by Boston merchants in the fur trade of the northern Pacific across to China and back with Chinese goods. Salem ships traded to the East Indies.

Maritime New England was adversely affected by the long European wars of the late 18th and early 19th centuries and by the war with Britain between 1812 and 1815, though the Pacific trade benefited from the absence of British competition. During these years speed to avoid capture by war vessels or privateers was often at a premium in the trades commanded by United States vessels. Perhaps too, circumstances led builders to be less affected by the restrictions of tonnage measurement rules on vessel design than appears to have been the case in Britain. After the war New England investors began to turn to some extent from the sea to the development of industry on land. The coasting trade with cotton and timber from the southern states began to grow and was confined to United States-built and enrolled vessels by a law of 1817 which is still in force and which, as we shall see later, was to have great effect on the final development of the wooden sailing vessel.

American trade with the Baltic, China, the Mediterranean, the East and West Indies, South America and the South Seas, slowly began to return in the 1820s. Boston remained the principal port for the East India, Baltic and Mediterranean trades and Massachusetts remained the leading shipowning state until New York exceeded it in the early 1840s. By the 1840s American merchant shipping was in the full tide of prosperity, with Baltimore and Philadelphia fleets rapidly expanding, in addition to those of New England and New York. Wherever they went British vessels in the 1840s were liable to find themselves in competition with similar vessels from the United States, not only from the great ports but from small places as well. Some of them were family concerns with the master's wife and children on board. With such a travelling home, often partly his own property, the master had the greatest possible incentive to maximise his revenue from freights.

By 1833, for example, it has been estimated that nearly three-quarters of the cotton imported into Great Britain arrived in American vessels. This was a triangular trade; vessels from the northern ports loaded with New England lumber and sometimes European goods made coastwise passages south where they discharged and loaded cotton for Europe at Charleston in South Carolina or at Savannah, Georgia, or New Orleans. They returned from Europe to the northern ports with manufactured goods from Great Britain and the Continent, or with coal, iron and salt.

Despite American shipbuilders' readiness to build fast vessels when the circumstances of trade made such vessels profitable, as in Britain the very similar tonnage measurement rules of the United States and the general conditions of trade influenced the form of the ordinary merchant vessel. A typical American merchant ship of the 1830s and 40s was long, narrow, and deep and very similar to the *Superb* in general hull form. She might carry a cargo amounting to nearly twice her registered tonnage, but she was a poor sailer, locally known in New England as a 'kettle bottom', her midships section almost rectangular and her ends short and full. The type can clearly be seen today in the whaler *Charles W Morgan*, built at New Bedford in 1841 and now preserved at Mystic, Connecticut, the last merchant ship in the world of the classic type which made up the bulk of the world's fleets for the first half of the 19th century.

# The New Ships, 1850-1865

The period covered by this chapter has been called the great age of the clipper ship. It was indeed, as we shall see, a period when for good commercial reasons it paid to utilise and develop the well-established shipbuilding traditions for the construction of fast merchant vessels which had long existed on both sides of the Atlantic.

In Britain the introduction, in Acts of Parliament of 1836 and 1854, of new methods of measuring tonnage which did not give economic advantage in terms of low dues based on tonnage to deep, narrow, long, full-bodied vessels with full ends, made commercially possible the building of better designed vessels, handier, more stable and generally likely to sail faster. Nevertheless, the numbers of especially fast vessels were very limited at any one time in relation to the total number of merchant ships at sea and they represented a small percentage of total maritime activity. The majority of merchant sailing vessels changed only very slowly as the changing pattern of trade and commerce made different types of vessel more profitable. On the whole during this period the ordinary merchant ship became larger, shallower, and sharper in hull form than her predecessors. Partly because ships were larger, partly because they were better designed, the general level of sailing performance improved and in a few special trades became spectacular.

Sailing vessel development involved three principal elements. These were cargo capacity, a factor of both shape and size, bigger vessels were cheaper to run per ton mile than smaller ones and were on the whole faster; speed, because the more ton miles sailed per year the greater the profitability; and operating costs, the latter historically very difficult indeed to calculate for merchant sailing vessels. The majority of trades of this period, for example, lumber from Canada to Britain, wheat from San Francisco to Liverpool, rice from Burma to London, iron rails to any developing country, did not require any special speed because only a limited number of passages could be made in a year and it was profitable to carry big cargoes. Fast vessels were limited to premium freights – soft fruit from the Azores to London because it was perishable, tea from China to London or New York because of the workings of this particular commodity market, goods and people from New York to San Francisco because the West coast was booming after the discovery of gold and the quicker investment could be made there, the more profitable it was likely to be, goods and people from Britain to Australia during the gold rush of the early 1850s, passengers and small freight parcels between New York and Liverpool, on which route fast vessels had been sailing to some sort of schedules since the 1820s, because business men (as opposed to the mass of emigrants) wanted to move backwards and forwards across the Atlantic with the minimum loss of working time.

Admittedly it is a simplification, but the true importance of the much romanticised clipper can be expressed in one statistic. In 1860 the total gross tonnage of sailing ships registered at home ports in the United Kingdom was about 4 200 000. In the same year at a generous estimate the vessels which might fairly be classed as clippers which loaded the season's tea in Chinese ports for Britain (and it was

These photographs demonstrate very clearly the general nature of the changes away from traditional forms and materials which took place in merchant sailing vessel construction in the 1850s and '60s.

Plate 9 The brig *Mitchelgrove* (so spelled on her stern but not always by her contemporaries) of Littlehampton was built within the limits of the Port of Arundel in 1815. With her very full lines, heavy transom counter, and thick hemp shrouds and stays she epitomises the ordinary small merchant vessel of the first half of the 19th century.
Photo: National Maritime Museum

Plate 10 The snow *Emma* was of approximately the same size as the *Mitchelgrove* and was built within the same port area but in 1866, when this photograph was taken. She has relatively fine lines, especially at the stern, is beamier and shallower, and has thin iron wire shrouds and stays. She was launched for the River Plate trade, which, because of the tortuous nature of the channels, was one of many 19th-century trades employing small vessels.
Photo: National Maritime Museum

a good year for freights) totalled under 20 000 tons gross, less than half of one per cent of the total tonnage of British merchant ships sailing from home ports alone. Even if you add in all the other vessels employed in branches of merchant shipping in which speed was profitable – coastal packets, fruit schooners, trans-Atlantic packets and fast vessels in other trades it is unlikely they add up to more than two per cent of the total, perhaps a slightly higher percentage of American tonnage. Yet more has been written and published about this minute percentage than about the whole of the rest of the world's tonnage put together and a much distorted picture of the development of the sailing vessel and the world's merchant shipping industries generally, has, as a result, become part of popular mythology.

Most vessels built for definite trades had one or more peculiarities which rendered them inefficient in other trades. The best merchant sailing vessels were those which rated high on all the three principal factors and had good cargo capacity, reasonable speed and low operating costs. During this period of the 1850s and early 60s the ordinary square-rigged wooden merchant vessel came nearest to attaining these qualities (Plates 9 and 10).

This was a period of unprecedented industrial development when Britain was moving towards the summit of economic power. The boom of 1854-55, triggered off by the Crimean War, affected shipping particularly and, with its post-war bankruptcies and disasters, was succeeded by two decades of expansion, consequent upon the extension of currency and credit based on the Californian and Australian gold discoveries, the repeal of the Navigation Acts which gave to British seafarers the stimulus of much stronger foreign competition, the passing of the Companies Act of 1861 which encouraged greater risk taking, the general development of banking, the spread of settlement in North America and the steadily developing industrialisation of the north east of the United States, and the development of railways on both sides of the Atlantic. United Kingdom registered sailing vessel tonnage increased by 23 per cent from 3 400 000 in 1850 to 4 200 000 in 1860. Steam tonnage, still confined to packet routes, tugs, short sea bulk carriers and subsidised deep sea routes, increased in the same decade from 170 000 net tons to 450 000 net tons.

During the same period, United States sailing vessel tonnage in overseas, coastal and lakes trades, increased from 2 900 000 to 4 400 000. The American expansion, stimulated by industrialisation and the opening up of the west coast, was largely in world wandering wooden square-rigged vessels, many of them built in New England. The brig, barque or full-rigged ship, built and owned perhaps in some small settlement in Maine between the Kennebeck and the Passamaquoddy with the master's wife and family on board, with local officers and as far as possible a local crew, was to be met with all over the world (Plate 11). Standards of maintenance, management, seamanship and navigation were high, as was the reputation of American ships and their masters in the international community of merchant shipping. The expansive economic climate of the United States was such that, despite the operation of their own tonnage measurement rules, which continued to benefit long, narrow, deep vessels until 1864, fast vessels were built for special trades rather earlier than in Britain, chiefly as a result of the opening up and rapid development of the west coast. Because of the long years in which American vessels had had to depend on speed to escape their numerous enemies there was a strong tradition for fast sailing hulls, as there was also for the weatherly schooner rig.

At the same time the Canadian shipbuilding industry was steadily growing. Between the years

1850 and 1865 inclusive, 846 wooden sailing vessels and one steamer were built in Quebec, averaging 722 tons each, the largest of over 2000 tons and many of them over 1500 tons. As is to be expected, the peak years, 1854 and 1864, coincide with the Crimean and American Civil War booms. Nova Scotian vessels were built on the whole not for sale to Britain but for operation from Canada, and by the middle of the 1860s Nova Scotian-owned ships with masters from the home area who held shares, managed and sailed very much like the American vessels of the period, began to be a significant factor in the world's carrying trade. Over the same period it was unusual for a wooden vessel built in Britain to exceed 1000 tons. Thus in terms of tonnage the size of the largest

British-built ordinary merchant ships roughly doubled between 1820 and 1860. But for the real economies of scale in an expanding economy British shipowners had to turn to Canadian builders, with their 1500 to 2000 tonners.

The growing merchant fleets of a Europe slower to industrialise than Britain also showed the influence of the long period of expansion of the 50s and early 60s. Norway's merchant fleet grew from 300 000 to 560 000 tons, France's from 675 000 to 930 000; in both cases almost all of the increase was in wooden sailing vessels. In Scandinavia and Russia successive laws were passed reflecting a gradual change from the principles of mercantilism, state power based on absolute monarchy and the granting of shipping

Plate 11  The new barque *Alden Besse*, built by Guy C. Goss, lies alongside the yard at Bath, Maine, in 1871. She differs from the vessels of ten years earlier mainly in having double topsails and topgallants. Her master was William H. Besse and the vessel under construction may be the three-masted schooner *Jesse Murdock* which was built for Mr Alden Besse in the same year. Note the team of oxen used for moving the big timbers around the yard. Photo: W.J. Lewis Parker

monopolies to the merchants of the towns. No longer was 'peasant sailing' by vessels not registered at the great ports strictly limited geographically.

In Finland, then a Grand Duchy of Russia, for instance, the blockade of the Gulfs of Bothnia and Finland by an Anglo-French fleet during the Crimean War resulted in the extensive sale of Finnish vessels outside the Baltic – fortunately often for good prices because of the world wide war boom. These sales were quickly replaced in the years after the peace, but in the intervening period extended privileges, which were never subsequently withdrawn, were given to peasant skippers, partly to make good the temporary deficiency in deep sea tonnage and partly as part of a movement towards greater individual freedom apparent generally in northern Europe at the period. Immediately, the shipping industry of the Åland Islands, where there was no town, began to develop. The Ålanders seventy-five years later were to be one of the last two western communities in history to operate big deep sea sailing vessels.

The 'Sound dues', taxes levied by the Danish authorities on the cargoes of all vessels passing into or out of the Baltic through the Sound between Helsingør and Helsingborg, were withdrawn in 1857 after prolonged international negotiations. There was something of an explosion of merchant shipping enterprise in northern Europe after this development, and the small wooden brig, brigantine, schooner or barque from the Åland Islands, Lübeck, Danzig, Memel, from south Sweden or the Finnish coast of Bothnia, and from Sønderborg, Drammen, Göteborg and Blankensee among other places, soon began to be met with all over the world (Plate 16). The schooner rig became more and more common. In the 1830s in Nova Scotia, and perhaps more or less simultaneously on the Elbe, the last of the classic merchant sailing ship rigs, the efficient and eco-nomical barquentine, was developed and rapidly gained favour on both sides of the Atlantic. Small Baltic vessels with the fore and aft ketch rig, sometimes with square topsails, the rig known as galease in Denmark, a type which had been in wide use since the 18th century, were more and more seen in British waters, on the Atlantic coast of France, and in the Mediterranean, and the ketch rig began to come into favour in the ports the vessels visited. It was to be separately evolved again on the west coast of Britain in the 1870s.

In Britain the period was one of continuous government legislation to improve the merchant shipping industry. Steady reforming pressure was applied. It was now seen as a function of Government to regulate the industry and from 1850 to 1906 scarcely a year passed in which a Committee or a Commission was not sitting or an Act of Parliament was not in course of preparation, or on its way through the House. Masters' and mates' qualifications, food, the manning of vessels, the draft to which they could be loaded, and increasingly the very structure and maintenance of the vessels themselves, came under regulation. The process was to come to its climax later in the Merchant Shipping Act of 1894, still the longest Act on the Statute Book.

All over the world charting improved, lighthouse services were established and other aids to navigation in restricted waters were introduced. But perhaps the greatest change of the period was that which followed the beginnings of the introduction of the international electric telegraph in the 1850s. The effect on merchant shipping was to be profound. No longer was the first news of a vessel's safe arrival overseas conveyed often by that same vessel on her return home. No longer was the Master's limited information on the state of the freight market necessarily confined to the port in which he had arrived. When a vessel arrived in port, not only had arrangements

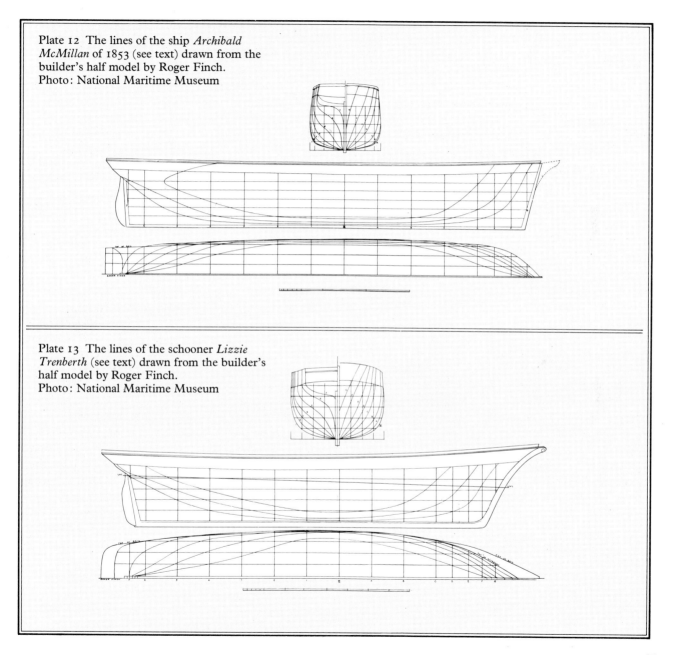

Plate 12 The lines of the ship *Archibald McMillan* of 1853 (see text) drawn from the builder's half model by Roger Finch.
Photo: National Maritime Museum

Plate 13 The lines of the schooner *Lizzie Trenberth* (see text) drawn from the builder's half model by Roger Finch.
Photo: National Maritime Museum

been made to discharge her cargo but her subsequent movements were likely to have been agreed. In short, the Master received his 'orders' as soon as he berthed his vessel. This revolution greatly increased the proportion of the vessel's life which was spent in gainful employment. The whole technique of the world commodity markets was changed and the commodity market in the modern sense began to emerge. Sea carrying power could now be mobilised and organised and the flow of international commerce enormously facilitated.

Plate 14 The brigantine *Sela*, launched in 1859, was typical of many dozen vessels of this type built in Prince Edward Island, Canada, for sale in the United Kingdom between the 1850s and the early 20th century. The *Sela* was the last Prince Edward Island-built sailing vessel to survive in Britain. Her hulk was broken up at Milford Haven in 1976 and ironwork then salved can be seen at the shipyard of the Shipbuilding Museum at Port Hill, Prince Edward Island. This photograph, taken from the only known print, shows the stamp of a once famous New York ship photographer, Edwin Levick.
Photo: Mariner's Museum, Newport News

The consequence of this complex general economic and social revolution in Britain, Europe and North America was a demand for different types of merchant vessels. No longer were ships confined to a limited range of often seasonal trades; something like a world freight market began to emerge. Increasingly, time began to represent money. Higher standards began to be demanded for the proper combination of reasonable speed, good cargo capacity, and low operating costs for the overwhelming majority of the world's ordinary merchant ships.

Generally speaking, the vessel which emerged on both sides of the Atlantic from this period of change was shallower, beamier, and sharper than the old ships. To illustrate the change I have chosen two vessels of approximately the same size as the *Superb* and the *Victoria* which illustrate the hull forms of the old ships. The *Archibald McMillan* (Plate 12) was built in 1853, early in the period covered by this chapter, for the West Indies trade. Described by her builders as a 'clipper' at a time when it was beginning to be fashionable to use the term, she is a typical good merchant vessel of the period and the differences between her shape and proportions and those of the *Superb* are too obvious to need comment. Similarly, the schooner *Lizzie Trenberth* (Plate 13) built in 1867 in Cornwall and employed initially in the Azores soft fruit trade, later in general trades, but representative of the hull form of many schooners constructed in the 1850s and 60s, presents a marked contrast with the *Victoria* of thirty years earlier and is the result of the application of quite different traditions of vessel design which became relevant in the changed economic conditions of the early part of the second half of the century.

In the late 1850s and the 60s the shipbuilding industry in Prince Edward Island found a ready market in Britain for brigantine-rigged vessels carrying 200 to 400 tons of cargo which were used in trade all over the Atlantic basin and further afield. In fact, vessels of this type continued to be built in steadily reducing numbers until the end of the century (Plate 14).

Besides the differences in hull shape—not new developments but the application of long known and well-established principles of vessel design applied when circumstances made them profitable—some of the new ships were of 'composite' construction, that is, built partly of iron with frames, or part of the frames, and perhaps stem and stern post of metal, with metal knees and straps. In the 1850s and 60s a

Plate 15 The barque *William Yeo* was built at Port Hill, Prince Edward Island, in 1862 for William Yeo of Apple-dore, Devon, and his father James Yeo and brother James Yeo Jr of Port Hill. Typical of her type and period she demonstrates a stage in the transition from single to double topsails, with the former on her mizzen and the latter on her fore and main. A few years after this picture was made by J.Semple in 1867 the yards were stripped from her mizzen and she was rigged as a barque. Employed in general ocean trade, but particularly in the Canadian timber trade to Britain, the *William Yeo* was lost in 1896 when under Norwegian ownership.
Photo: National Maritime Museum

few merchant sailing vessels were built entirely of iron and I shall refer to these in the next chapter.

As well as experiments with the main fabric of the ship, many improvements were made on deck and in the rigging. In place of the simple windlass heaved around with hand spikes which had been in use since the 16th century at least, the 'Patent' windlass converting an up-and-down motion of levers into the rotary motion of the barrel was introduced and remained in large vessels until steam donkey engine power took over, and in small vessels until the ultimate end of the sailing ship in the mid-20th century. Anchor cranes, brace and sheet winches, better cargo-handling gear, improved pumps, iron lower masts and even lower yards, the widespread use of iron wire for standing and some running rigging, spread very slowly as materials became commercially cheaply available and their demonstrable advantages overcame intense conservatism. Some old schooners and ketches were still sailing with hemp standing rigging in the 20th century.

In the 1850s double topsails, sometimes only on fore and main (Plate 15), began to appear in place of the huge and uncontrollable, if beautiful, single topsails, which had persisted since the late 1400s, and double topgallants were soon to follow. Better mast iron work and the steadily improving qualities of fabric readily and cheaply available for the sails themselves greatly increased their efficiency.

All these developments made it possible to build bigger and more efficient schooners, because with better ironwork, iron wire standing rigging, improved blocks, improved natural fibre rope for the running rigging, and improved canvas, the problem of setting big gaff sails efficiently was almost solved. At the end of the period the schooner was on the verge of a great leap forward in development which was later to prolong the life of the merchant sailing ship all over the world for a full generation.

Nevertheless the years 1850 to 1865 were the heyday of the wooden square-rigged merchant sailing ship (Plate 16). Especially if she was built at comparatively low cost in labour and materials in Canada, she represented by far the cheapest way of carrying goods at sea (Plate 17). The steamship, after 50 years of experiment and development, could not match her economically and was still confined to short sea and subsidised routes and special trades. The wooden barque, the brig, the brigantine, the full-rigged ship, the two-masted schooner with square topsails on the foremast of the type illustrated in Plate 22, were the carriers of blossoming world trade. But they were very bad insurance risks.

An examination of the contemporary shipping press shows day after day reports of ships in every kind of major distress. Often the reports are of mysterious total disasters which could never be explained. A vessel, evidently of American construction, is ashore, upside down, on Hartland Point, North Devon, with only her lower timbers remaining. A vessel, evidently a schooner, is seen upside down in the Caribbean, sea too rough to approach closely. A fishing schooner, with only her main lower mast standing, is sighted awash off Cape Cod. There are no signs of life and her name cannot be read. The master of a barque arriving in Sydney reports laconically that he and his crew sighted a burning ship in the South Atlantic weeks before. There were no signs of life and the vessel could not be identified.

Statistics have not yet been seriously examined, but it seems not unlikely that the wooden square-rigged sailing ship, ambling about the coasts and over the seas of the world at an average speed, if she was well designed and equipped, well commanded and well managed, of about five miles an hour, and more especially the fast wooden sailing ship sailed fast, was probably the most dangerous vehicle ever regularly used by man.

Plate 16 (left) The harbour of Maryport, Cumbria, filled with wooden vessels of the 1850s, when this photograph was taken.
Photo: National Maritime Museum

Plate 17 (below) The barque *Asta* was built at Maitland, Nova Scotia, and was owned in Norway at Farsund when this photograph of her was taken off Portishead in the Bristol Channel. She is outward bound from Bristol or Gloucester and is towing the cutter of the Cardiff pilot who is taking her down the difficult waterway. Denny Island is visible between her fore and main masts.
Photo: National Maritime Museum

# The Industrial Revolution goes to sea, 1865-1909

By 1865 the steamship was at last developed to a point at which it could successfully compete with sailing vessels. From this year onwards the demise of the sailing vessel was certain. What was uncertain was how long it would take her to die.

In fact, under the stimulus of competition from steamships which she had previously escaped, with the encouragement provided by the removal of the British merchant shipping industry's most serious rival, the United States, and with the opportunities provided by prolonged industrial and commercial development over the next 30 years, the big sailing vessel was changed and developed out of all recognition, so that in the 1890s and very early 1900s the last of them to be built bore almost no resemblance in structure, efficiency or even appearance, to the majority of the vessels so far described and illustrated in this book. The small sailing vessel changed less; nonetheless she too went through a remarkable development in efficiency, economy and even safety.

To understand what happened it is necessary to look briefly at the industrial histories of Britain and the United States in the first decades of the second half of the century. Professor Gerald Graham has written of the 'incredible defiance of the industrial revolution by sail during the second half of the 19th century'. This paradox of a machine brought by investment to its greatest efficiency in design when it was clearly obsolete was partly the result of the inevitable slowness of the development of processes of manufacturing cheap iron, and later steel, of the quality and size essential to enable boilers to be made which would stand the pressures necessary to make the marine steam engine economical enough in fuel consumption to leave the steamship with sufficient room to carry cargo to pay her way.

For the progress of the steamship in the 19th century is the progress of the iron and steel industries. It is as well to remember that the paddle steamer could never be efficient and economical in general ocean trade, while the wooden screw steamer rapidly tore herself to pieces because of torque and other stresses. Only the iron screw steamer could survive. But the production and use of iron in the sizes and quantities and at the prices needed for shipbuilding really only began at the time of the *Great Britain* in the early 1840s. In 1850, 120000 tons of wooden shipping and 12800 tons of iron ships were built in Britain. In 1860 the corresponding figures were 147000 tons of wooden shipping and 64700 tons of iron shipping, including some fine big iron sailing vessels (Plate 18). Not until 1870 was the figure reversed, as iron became better and cheaper and the marine steam engine had made the great leap forward which will be described in the next paragraph. In that year a total of 161000 tons of wooden shipping were built in Britain, together with 255000 tons of iron shipping, including many first class sailing vessels. By 1880 in Britain, only small sailing vessels were being built of wood and of the half million gross tons of iron shipping built, only about one-fifth represents sailing tonnage.

For by then the availability of good cheap iron had made possible the third major and revolutionary development in the steam vessel. To recapitulate, the first great development was screw propulsion,

Plate 18 The iron barque *Montrosa*
*ex Montrose* built at Glasgow in 1863,
one of the earlier iron sailing vessels, was
employed by her first British owners in the
Australian trade. In 1885 she was sold to
German owners and in 1898 to owners in
Lemland, Åland. From this small Baltic
island she sailed all over the world for
thirty years until she was broken
up in 1929. Photo: National
Maritime Museum

the second was iron construction, and the third was an economical engine. All steam vessels until the 1850s were driven by simple engines, that is, single-cylinder machines into which steam was injected at pressures developing gradually from about 5 lbs per square inch in the 1830s to about 20 lbs per square inch in the 1850s, because in each decade boilers could not be built from commercially available iron to withstand higher working pressures. The steam was used once only and then condensed back into water for reheating. Most of the energy of the expanding steam was wasted, hence the vast quantities of fuel needed, hence the small cargo carried and hence the fact that the steam vessel could not compete in ocean trade with the sailing vessel without a subsidy. Full-sized simple engines of the side lever type developed for paddle steamer use can be seen in the National Maritime Museum in the tug *Reliant*, and a small simple engine for screw propulsion in the steam launch *Waterlily* in the same gallery of the Museum.

For years it had been known that much more power could be developed for the same consumption of fuel if steam could be used a second time, expanding further, in a second, bigger, cylinder after it had passed through the first small high-pressure cylinder. Experiments on these lines in France and America in the early 19th century had always ended in failure, principally because of the difficulty of generating steam at sufficient pressures to enable such a system to be worked. But in 1856 the Pacific Steam Navigation Company successfully operated two vessels with compound engines. A few years later Alfred Holt of Liverpool, a civil engineer by training who had become a businessman and shipowner, installed and operated an improved compound engine in one of his ships. Its success led him in 1865 to build (in a yard right alongside one building tea clippers of iron frames and wooden planks) three iron steamers each fitted with compound engines so small and so efficient that the vessel could carry a cargo of 3000 tons, two or three times as much as almost all contemporary sailing vessels, and at the same time sufficient coal to drive her at a steady 10 miles an hour for 8500 miles without refuelling. It is most unlikely in fact that she ever did so, since it would have been more profitable to carry more cargo and no more fuel than that demanded by the distance between bunkering ports on her trade routes.

The secret lay largely with the boilers. Iron was now available of such quality, and boiler-building techniques had developed to such a degree, that steam pressures of 60 lb per square inch could be achieved. The coal consumption of these vessels was as little as $2\frac{3}{4}$ lb per hour per ton, less than a quarter of that of early steamers. Small examples of compound engines can be seen in the steam launch *Donola* and also on separate display in the National Maritime Museum.

The new steamers were put immediately into the China trade and since they could travel to and fro regularly in 64 days against the crack sailing ship time of an uncertain 90 days and could carry three times the cargo, it was in this high freight, prestigious trade that the making of an end to the merchant sailing ship was at last begun. At long last, in the very year, 1865, when Canadian shipbuilders produced more tonnage than ever for British owners and the wooden square-rigged merchant sailing vessel was completely dominant in world trade, she was suddenly, after almost five centuries of use, rendered obsolete. As R.H. Thornton put it, writing of tea clippers, in his study *British Shipping* in 1939, 'From the year 1863 to 1869 British yards went on turning out an unimpeachable series of these little 800 ton yachts, like *Taeping*, *Serica*, *Ariel*, *Sir Lancelot*, *Thermopylae* and *Cutty Sark*, mostly to the order of thoroughly conservative ex-captain owners and destined for a trade (the China tea trade) which was already as good as lost. . . . What was the use of the clipper, when the cargo steamer was already born?'

Some 10 years later the building of big wooden sailing ships in Britain had virtually ceased. The Canadian and United States industries continued for longer. Cheap, well-built Canadian wooden tonnage enjoyed something of a boom in the early 1870s and many fine big square-rigged vessels were built for operation by Nova Scotian owners. In the 1870s big three-masted schooners were built in Prince Edward Island for operation by British owners in the trade round Cape Horn to the West coast of South America, and in the 1880s a type of efficient bulk-carrying barquentine was developed in the same yards. The building of wooden barques continued on a small scale in Sweden and Finland into the 1890s. The only wooden three-masted cargo-carrying merchant sailing vessel to survive in the world in her original configuration is one of these late Swedish barques, the *Sigyn* of Vårdö, built at Göteborg in 1887 and now preserved at Åbo in Finland, the property of the Swedish-speaking university, the Åbo Akademi. She is a very good example of a late wooden square-rigged ship, and to visit her and examine her accommodation is to enter a forgotten world (Plate 19).

The opening of the Suez Canal in 1869 has often been quoted as the turning point in the life of the sailing vessel, but this contention is not supported by the facts. The indication that the turning point had come had already been given four years before. True, the opening of the Canal in a situation rendered fraught for sailing ship owners by the success of the compound engine gave a check for a year or two to the building of sailing vessels of either wood or iron in Britain. Before the compound engine the Canal would not have mattered because even with a saving of 5000 miles on the route to the east the simple-

engined steamer using the Canal could still not have been competitive with the sailing vessel going round the Cape. But the compound-engined steam vessel could use the Canal with great profit, and simple calculations showed that the sailing vessel would not be able to compete in the bulk of the contemporary Indian trades. So, in a situation of uncertainty, the building of all big sailing vessels in Britain almost stopped and in 1871 very few were launched, while the output of steam tonnage, now with compound engines, was almost twice as big as ever before.

But, paradoxically, in the crucial year of 1865, another event took place which in complex and different ways was to play a part in prolonging the life of the sailing vessel. The American Civil War came to an end, leaving a triumphant industrial north and a shattered rural south. Four years later, in the same year as the opening of the Suez Canal, an

Plate 19 The carved and gilded decorative woodwork on the stern and starboard quarter of the wooden barque *Sigyn* of Wårdö or Vårdö, built at Göteborg in 1887. Now preserved at Åbo, in Finland, she is the last wooden three-masted square-rigged merchant sailing ship in the world.
Photo: Lars Grönstrand

event even more important in world history than the opening of the Canal was the completion of the transcontinental railroad across North America. Now, with a great financial and industrial base in the north-east and a stable political situation, the continent could at last be opened up.

No society, no men or women, turn to the sea as a means of life if there is any acceptable alternative on land. To make a life on the sea one needs to be pushed. During the Civil War nearly half the American deep water merchant fleet had been destroyed, sold, or transferred to foreign flags. After the war it was obvious that the future of shipping lay with iron and steel and steam, but the high local cost of the former prohibited the building of a modern merchant fleet of steamships in North America. A United States law effectively forbade the building up of a merchant fleet by the purchase of foreign-built tonnage. Rapid industrialisation and phenomenal population growth through massive emigration absorbed most American manufactured products, so there was relatively little export trade for American ships to carry. Money and men turned from the sea to industry, railroads, real estate and the west. The west provided trades in which the big wooden square-rigged sailing vessel lingered for another decade or so. It was still profitable for United States shipowners to carry grain from California, Washington and Oregon to Europe and for this and complementary trades big square-rigged ships, the 'down easters', continued to be built in numbers totalling between two and three hundred in Maine until 1885 (Plate 20). Until the mid-1870s the carriage of guano from the Chincha Islands off Peru to Europe and

Plate 20 The New England 'down easter' *A G Ropes*, launched in 1884 by Chapman & Ropes at Bath, Maine. Typical of this class of tonnage, with channels to spread the shrouds and backstays, fully enclosed wheelhouse at a time when such luxuries were virtually unknown in British ships, long aftercabin sunk into the poop deck, and big deckhouse fo'c'sle, she was considered one of the two or three finest of the last generation of big wooden square-rigged sailing vessels built in the United States. Photo: National Maritime Museum

Eastern North America provided many cargoes for American sailing vessels. Cargoes of case oil carried in square-rigged sailing vessels from North America to the Far East were complemented by cargoes of sugar from Java and manilla rope fibres from the Philippines. Barrelled oil was carried to Europe in considerable numbers of American wooden sailing vessels.

Nevertheless, the British merchant shipping industry lost its most serious competitor. Meanwhile by the early 1870s, world trade was recovering after the temporary set back of the post-American Civil War slump. World industrial expansion and the development of routes for compound-engined steamers were based on coal as fuel and Britain was the world's largest exporter – the Persian Gulf of the last quarter of the 19th century. So there was always outward cargo for a British sailing vessel, a ballast on which freight was paid, and she took bulk products home. Increasingly it was to be an asset to a sailing vessel to be 'the cheapest warehouse in the world', to provide virtually free storage for cargoes which changed hands on the commodity markets many times while she made a long passage. Hence, given an economy generally expanding over time, the sailing vessel was to continue to be a reasonable investment for British shipowners for about a generation after the beginning of large scale building of compound-engined steamships and British shipyards were to build many hundreds of big iron and steel square-rigged vessels until the final collapse of the market for new sailing tonnage in 1897.

Coal was exported to the Pacific ports of South America in these British ships, nitrate brought back to Europe. The massive delivery to European markets of grain from the wheat lands of the American west, carried to the coast on the new railroads, was made possible almost entirely by sailing vessels which had carried coal out to San Francisco. In 1882

550 big sailing vessels were engaged in this trade. These were largely British vessels with some of the American 'down easters' already referred to and some Canadian-owned wooden ships. Australian grain exports increased by $2\frac{1}{2}$ times between the mid-1870s and the end of the 1880s. Coal, manufactured goods and emigrants went out to Australia in sailing vessels, grain and wool came back to Europe in the same ships. In the 1870s, while the compound steam engine was steadily establishing itself, and the world wide pattern of coaling stations was beginning to be built up, the sailing vessel took coal out to the eastern bunkering ports, rice or jute home from Calcutta; she carried iron rails, much in demand for the world's expanding railway systems, at great danger to herself, especially if she was a wooden ship, anywhere they had to be delivered.

Plate 21 The British three-masted schooner *Frau Minna Petersen*, later renamed *Jane Banks*, was built at Porthmadog in 1878 for the salt fish trade from Newfoundland and the slate trade to Europe, especially to German ports. A classic vessel of her type she survived generations of technical change to be lost in the Gulf of Finland in 1944.
Photo: National Maritime Museum

In the home trade the brig, and even the brigantine, gave way after 1870 to the efficient, economical, three-masted schooner with square topsails on her foretopmast, a vessel carrying up to 250 tons of cargo (Plate 21). The ketch was reinvented, in the West of England at least, because the demand for larger vessels, even in the most domestic of trades, led to the lengthening of the old coasting smacks and the addition of a little mizzen mast to give them the bigger sail area they now needed (Plate 22). For those

Plate 22 The schooner *Colleen*, built at Barnstaple in 1880, and the ketch *Humility*, built at Littlehampton in 1839 with point reefing and jackyard topsail set from aloft in the classic 19th century style, being towed to sea from Appledore in North Devon by the tug *Times*. The ketch *Acacia*, built at Plymouth in 1880, is nearest the camera, sailing down towards the Bar. She has roller reefing and a jib headed topsail set on a jackstay from the deck, labour-saving devices introduced in the early 20th century.
Photo: National Maritime Museum

trades all over the world, and particularly in the Atlantic Basin, which required small tonnage, three-masted schooners, small barquentines, and a few brigantines, were still built in some numbers in Britain and Canada and operated in trade to the Baltic, Mediterranean and particularly in the Newfoundland salt fish trade to Europe. For the big ships, iron hulls were soon followed by iron masts and yards and iron wire for standing and even for some running rigging. The endless pumping of the wooden ship was eliminated, maintenance work for the crews, though still formidable, was much reduced. Rigging was simplified, hulls became steadily more burdensome until with the availability of cheap iron in quantity and in the right sizes, the standard big sailing vessel of Britain became a three-masted barque or big full-rigged ship able to carry several times the cargo of the ordinary wooden sailing vessel of 1860 much more safely, with greatly increased cargo space in proportion to registered tonnage, and manned by a much smaller crew in proportion to tonnage.

Crews did not increase in size in step with the carrying capacity of the big vessel and the crews of small vessels became even smaller. What happened is illustrated by the fact that the full-rigged ship *Ocean Queen* of Bristol, 630 tons, built in 1845, sailing to Quebec from the Bristol Channel in 1855 had a total crew of 20, master, two mates, bosun, carpenter, steward, cook and 13 seamen. The crew of the wooden full-rigged ship *A J Fuller*, built in 1881, 1850 tons, with something like three times the cargo capacity of the *Ocean Queen*, on a passage from New York to California in 1897 comprised her master, two mates, a carpenter, 16 seamen and one boy, total of 21. A German four-masted barque of the 90s carrying 2 250 000 board feet of lumber from the West Coast of North America had a crew of 33 while the five-masted schooner *Crescent* in the same trade demonstrated a really great leap forward in sailing ship technology by carrying 1 654 000 board feet with a crew of ten. The crew of the little barque *Civility* in 1848 (page 10), 94 feet long, comprised 10 men. The crew of the British three-masted schooner *John Pritchard*, 92 feet long, in the North Atlantic trade in 1904 was exactly half the size.

In the United States the coastal trade continued not merely to provide employment for large numbers of sailing vessels, but to grow. Under legislation dating back to the early years of the 19th century foreign-flag vessels were not allowed to trade between American ports and neither were foreign-built vessels, even under the American flag. The coastal trade consequently enjoyed a prosperity which has continued to a certain extent to the present day, and after the Civil War a greater tonnage of American flag vessels was employed in coastwise than in foreign trades.

In the late 19th century the demands for coal for the new factories in New England, for the railroads and for domestic heating in the growing northern cities, and in due course for the production of domestic gas and electric power, all created a vast requirement for the product which could only be satisfied from the mines of Pennsylvania, Maryland and West Virginia. The transport of coal gave rise to an enormous demand for shipping, and it was in this trade that the American schooner really came of age.

Though two-masted schooners (Plate 23) persisted in use in local trade on the New England coast, as on the British coast, until the Second World War, in the 1860s and 70s the three-masted schooner became established in both British and United States waters, but the American schooners were much larger than the British, running up to a maximum cargo capacity of about 1100 tons. Even so, they were quite unable to carry coal shipments of the sizes which soon were in demand. The result was that four-masters began

to be built in 1880 and by the end of the decade were being designed with a carrying capacity of up to 2500 tons (Plate 24). Between 1870 and 1899, over 1500 big three-masted schooners and 181 four-masters were built in the Atlantic States. To meet expanding demands for the shipment of lumber and other cargoes on the west coast over the same period some 138 four-masters, 4 five-masters (Plate 25) and numerous three-masters were built.

The big schooner's greatest advantage was, of course, that she was economical of man power,

Plate 23 The American two-masted schooner *Mary E Lynch* was built at Newcastle, Maine, in 1890 for the West Indies fruit trade to New England. Latterly she was employed in the granite trade from eastern Maine to Boston and New York City. It will be noted she has points reefing. American schooners were never fitted with the roller reefing gear which greatly reduced the labour of reefing in later British vessels with this rig. Photo: National Maritime Museum

Plate 24 The four-masted schooner *Bertha L Downs* shown just before her launch at Bath, Maine, in 1908, was one of the finest vessels of her class, exceptionally strongly built and well equipped. The photograph shows the powerful hull with sweeping sheer characteristic of these big New England schooners. She survived 40 years of active life under United States, Danish, Finnish, Estonian, Russian and German owners.
Photo: Bath Marine Museum

especially after the steam donkey engine was introduced for hoisting sail, raising anchors, and working the pumps in 1879. The big four-master needed only three or four skilled people and five or six foremast hands to handle her. A British schooner carrying an eighth as much cargo as the four-master needed a crew half as big, a barque of the same cargo capacity as the four-masted schooner needed two or three times the crew, even in the 1880s, and they had to be almost all skilled seamen. Though their principal employments were in the long-range coasting trades with coal and lumber, some of the big American schooners roved the world following old trans-Atlantic and trans-Pacific routes.

Like the United States, but a little later, Canada turned her back on the sea; men of enterprise looked to land, industry and the west. But like the Americans, the Canadians retained one specialised deep water sailing ship. She was the 'tern schooner', the three-master with masts all the same height, used in the international trade to East Coast United States ports, to the West Indies and especially across the Atlantic to the Mediterranean with salted codfish from Nova Scotia and Newfoundland. These vessels were markedly smaller than the big American coal schooners but over 800 of them were built in Nova Scotia, New Brunswick, Quebec, Prince Edward Island and Newfoundland. In its final form around about 1910 the 'round stemmed tern' represented one of the last two distinct types of merchant sailing ship to be developed anywhere.

So in the 1870s something of a balance was established between compound-engined steam and sail. But in the early 1880s when the compound-engined vessel seemed to have settled at the limits of its possibilities another development established the steamship as the normal method of sea transport and with the exception of the big schooner in North American waters brought about the end of the build-

Plate 25 The wooden five-masted schooner *Inca* beating out of Puget Sound. Built at Port Blakeley, State of Washington, in 1896, the *Inca* is a typical big west coast schooner. Photo: Robert A. Weinstein

ing of new large sailing vessels within about 15 years. This second revolution had its preliminaries. Iron plates were cheap in the 1870s, but steel for ship-building was expensive. There was an enormous demand for steel for other industrial purposes, and particularly for railway development throughout the world. But by the end of the 1870s steel was being used for boilers and furnace construction and this meant that steam pressures could be increased, with further consequent improvement to the efficiency of the compound engine – and fuel consumption was reduced by more than 60 per cent.

And then on the 7 April, 1881 the steamship *Aberdeen* sailed from Plymouth towards Melbourne. She had an engine in which the steam, having done its work in the second cylinder of the compound engine, was admitted to a third cylinder, even larger

Plate 26 Although the 1890s in Britain were the era of the four-masted barque and the big steel full-rigged ship smaller vessels were still launched like the barque *Favell*, built at Bristol in 1895 and not broken up until 1937.
Photo: National Maritime Museum

Plate 27 The steel full-rigged ship *Grace Harwar*, built at Port Glasgow in 1889, seen shortened down in a strong wind. The fore upper topsail is being set and two men are aloft casting off the gaskets. Able to carry 3000 tons of cargo the *Grace Harwar* later became the last full-rigged merchant sailing ship in the western world to carry cargo at sea.
Photo: National Maritime Museum

than the second, and there completed its expansion. This process was made possible by the high steam pressure obtained from steel boilers and improved furnaces. Again, the National Maritime Museum has an example of this historic type of marine engine, which represents one of the major landmarks in industrial history.

The *Aberdeen* completed her passage to Melbourne in 42 days with 4000 tons of cargo and only one coaling stop, working at a steam pressure of 125 lbs per square inch. Within three years 150 lbs per square inch was achieved in new steamships. In 1885 the two-cylinder compound engine ceased to be built and triple-expansion engines working at 200 lbs per square inch shortly followed. By the beginning of the 1890s a tramp steamer could operate at 9 knots on a fuel consumption of half an ounce of coal per ton per mile steamed. This statistic has been put in vivid terms by Robin Craig – a first class cargo steamer of the late years of Queen Victoria's reign could carry one ton of cargo one mile using heat in her furnace equivalent to that generated by burning one sheet of high quality Victorian writing paper.

By the mid-1880s the steam vessel was as economical as the new sailing vessel, bearing in mind that she could make three passages and thus carry three tons of cargo to the latter's one. It was the production and use of steel good enough and cheap enough to manufacture commercially practicable high pressure boilers which sealed the end of the sailing ship. The obsequies were merely hastened by improved port facilities, water ballast, better cargo gear, the introduction of self-trimming and the exploitation by steamship owners of the economies of scale.

But it was still to be a lingering death. Shipbuilders and owners clung to wrought iron into the 1880s because it was readily available in the cheapest forms acceptable to Lloyds and the other classification organisations. There was a world demand for

British steel for every conceivable industrial purpose and little incentive to the industry to produce cheap steel plates for shipbuilding. So it was not until 1885 that steel produced by the Bessemer and Siemens processes began to be used widely.

The new material, with its greater strength for weight, led to a rapid augmentation of the size and carrying capacity of British merchant sailing ships and, though smaller vessels continued to be built into the 1890s (Plate 26), in the larger classes the 1500 to 2000 tons iron three-masted ship or barque became the 3000 or more tons four-masted barque or full-rigged ship carrying up to 5000 tons of cargo (Plate 27). These last great steel square-rigged vessels, though as a type they were built in numbers for only about 12 years, were remarkable pieces of engineering. Often over 300 feet long, with long square sections and full ends making up a burden-some but very strong and powerful hull (Plate 28), capable of being sailed at consistently high average

Plate 28 The original builder's lines and hull drawings of the steel four-masted barques *Afon Alaw* and *Afon Cefni* built by Alexander Stephens & Son at Glasgow in 1891 and 1892. These vessels were typical of the last years of big sailing vessel construction in Britain. Photos: National Maritime Museum

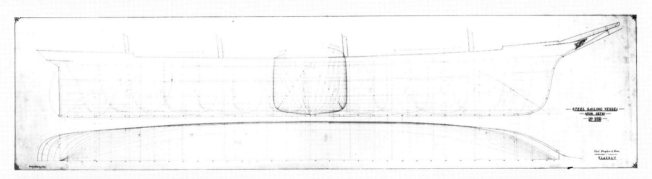

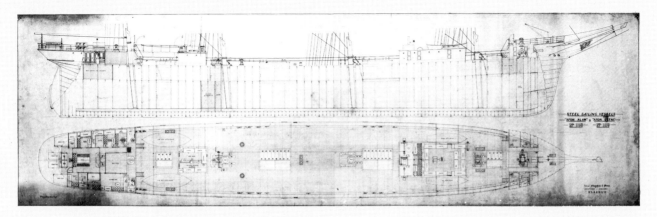

Plate 29 South West India Dock, London,
filled with iron and steel barques and
full-rigged ships in the late 1880s.
Photo: National Maritime Museum

Plate 30 Barry was the last of the great South Wales coal ports to be developed. This photograph was taken in the 1890s and shows steel and iron square-rigged sailings vessels congregated to load coal, while the steamer *Margaret Jones*, built at South Shields in 1889, illustrates the kind of triple expansion engined vessel with which the sailing vessel was able to compete for only a few more years, even in this bulk trade. Photo: National Maritime Museum

Plate 31 The watch taking in the mainsail on board the steel four-masted barque *Archibald Russell*, built at Greenock in 1905. Photo: Karl Kåhre

speeds if well handled, they represented for a few years a class of sailing tonnage which in some long range trades in years of prosperity could still give a reasonable return on capital, even in the world of the triple expansion-engined steamship. They were equipped with steam donkey engines which, by ingeniously devised belt transmissions, drove winches which lifted the huge lower yards to set the sails and powered the windlass to raise the anchors. Other labour-saving devices were developed – brace winches, halyard winches, labour-saving modifications to the running rigging. On the whole these latter improvements were ignored by British sailing ship owners, but they were taken up by German owners, some of whom for a short time in the early 20th century ran perhaps the finest square-rigged merchant sailing vessels ever to be at sea.

These last square-rigged British merchant vessels were built in the second half of the 1880s and the early 1890s, and especially during a shipping boom which lasted from 1888 to 1893 (Plate 29). There were over 250 of them. One shipyard on the Clyde alone built over sixty. These last vessels were employed in carrying guano and nitrate from South America, canned salmon and lumber from British Columbia, coal from Britain almost anywhere, grain from San Francisco to Liverpool, timber from Sweden to Australia, and grain back to Europe, timber from Puget Sound to Britain, jute from Calcutta, coal from Newcastle, New South Wales, to the West Coast of South America. There were over 100 four-masted barques as well as barques, full-rigged ships and a few beautiful and efficient steel four-masted barquentines amongst them. Together

steel hulls and fittings, required a shipyard for all major repairs. Masts and yards were no longer sent down in bad weather – the mainyard of a four-masted barque, a tapering steel tube, could be 90 feet long, two feet in diameter amidships and weigh several tons (Plate 31). The ships depended on structural strength to see them through. Their crews were not called upon to be skilled in the ways the men of the 1840s had been. The best portrait of a crew of a big vessel of this period is that drawn by Joseph Conrad in his sombre and powerful novel *The Nigger of the Narcissus*, which is also the best account of a passage in such a vessel ever written.

These new ships continued to be built in the 1890s because they could compete with steamships and offer reasonable return on investment in a few bulk cargo trades at a time of increasingly competitive freight rates and rising real costs of bunker coal. But in fact these vessels operated on the margins both of profits and of time and could survive only until a slight change in economic conditions took place.

By 1897 this had happened and the recovery in the freight market for steamships accompanying the outbreak of the Spanish–American and Boer Wars finally and permanently shifted the balance in favour of steam. In 1897 also a large and general increase in insurance costs at London for sail tonnage further weakened the position of sailing ship owners. The last little trickle of big square-rigged ships was launched between 1900 and 1906, some of them for German owners. The trickle ended with the *Mozart* and *Beethoven*, four-masted barquentines, the *Moshulu*, a four-masted barque, the *Archibald Russell*, a four-masted barque, and the barques *Sunlight* and *Rendova*. The new vessels of the 1890s had cost £22 000 or so each to build, depending on size, quality of construction, and date of build, say about £8.50p in modern currency per ton. By 1907 the same ships were reselling for £4.00 per ton and by

with the survivors of the 1870s, and of the era of the wooden ship, they made an enormous fleet of big British merchant sailing vessels still in operation all over the world in the early 1890s (Plate 30).

These vessels were not virtually self-supporting machines, as the old wooden ships had been. It was not possible for their crews to re-rig them after dismasting, replace their spars, repair their leaks and refit the vessels themselves. Steel masts and spars,

1910 for just over £2.00 per ton. With no construction the old ships were slowly run to death. With little capital to depreciate and no idea of setting aside funds to build new ships, a number of companies in Britain made sufficient profit to operate dwindling fleets until the First World War in the depressing conditions vividly described by Alan Villiers in *The War with Cape Horn*. Others were sold to German, Italian, Spanish, Norwegian and Åland owners who, because of peculiar social and economic circumstances (as in Åland) or less stringent state regulation, or in some cases superior management techniques, could make money with them in the world's carrying trade.

There was some small experimentation with new styles of rigging in the last years of the square-rigged sailing vessel on both sides of the Atlantic. The most

important of these, and the one which probably pointed the way to the future, had the big sailing ship survived at all, was the development of the big barquentine. The three-masted barquentine rig had been in use since the 1830s and was very successful in vessels of moderate tonnage in general trade. In the barquentine the two strands which run through this history, the development of the gaff-rigged vessel and that of the square-rigged vessel, are twisted together to make a unity with many of the merits of both. In the United States, and especially on the west coast, big wooden barquentines became popular in the early 1880s. They cost far less to build and sail than a ship or barque and they could run a schooner out of sight on an ocean passage.

The secret of the big barquentines, as of the big schooner, lay in keeping the gaff sails reasonably

Plate 32 (right) The steel four-masted barquentine *Mozart* was built at Greenock in 1904 as a cargo carrying training ship for Hamburg owners. She made excellent passages in the Chilean nitrate trade to Germany and in the trans-Pacific trades, operating with a crew of only 16 with 12 cadets. She was considerably bigger than most American five-masted schooners and her gaff sails must have been among the largest ever made. Like those of the big schooners they were set with the aid of a steam donkey engine.
Photo: National Maritime Museum

Plate 33 (far right) In 1921 *Mozart*–shown here running dead in the southern ocean in a photograph taken from the starboard mizzen rigging–was sold to Åland owners. She remained a profitable vessel but her crews of 18 or 19 (as opposed to the 23 or 24 required for a barque of the same deadweight tonnage) had endless work taking in and resetting the huge gaff sails to avoid expensive wear in adverse conditions of weather and sea. She would have been much handier and even more profitable as a five- or six-master. There is a fine model of this vessel with a deck cargo of timber in the National Maritime Museum.
Photo: Karl Kåhre

small by increasing the number of masts as the vessels grew bigger. One of the most successful of the last American square-rigged sailing ships was the six-masted barquentine *E R Sterling*. In Britain and Europe experiments made with big barquentines sometimes fell into the trap of too few masts for the size and consequently of gaff sails which were too big. The best known of these experiments was the British-built, German-owned, *Mozart* (Plates 32 and 33) a successful vessel financially, which survived to work at sea for over thirty years.

The big American wooden schooners on the East Coast had a different history from the last British steel sailing ships. The industrial boom which followed the Spanish–American war of 1898, with other factors, led to a great revival in the construction for the east coast coal and other trades. In the coal trade, which, despite their employment with many other types of cargo, remained the backbone of the operation of these big schooners, one of the big factors in favour of sailing vessels was the inadequacy of the facilities available at the coal loading ports and the irregularity with which the coal supplies came down to the wharves from the pits.

The trade had expanded too rapidly for railway and dock facilities to keep pace. Vessels were frequently delayed for a week, sometimes much more, waiting for loads. Schooners with their low overheads could afford these delays, steamers could not. In this trade vessels were loaded in strict order of arrival at the ports and through pressure and through legal action the schooner owners succeeded in maintaining this practice well into the 20th century. So the schooner continued to prosper and develop and took further steps forward, in competition with trains of towed barges in the coasting trade, with the beginning of the building on the East Coast of five-masters as late as 1898 and of six-masters two years later.

In 1909, however, the Virginia railway was opened for the sole purpose of transporting coal from new West Virginia fields to Norfolk for shipment. Its tidewater piers had the largest loading capacity in the world and brought to an end the delays in loading which had precluded the employment of steamers in the New England trade. The effect was as decisive as the events of 1897 had been on the steel square-rigged sailing vessels of Britain. In 1909 the launch of six four-masters and of the mighty *Wyoming*, the largest six-master and the second largest wooden merchant sailing vessel ever built, able to carry over 5000 tons of cargo, marked the end of schooner building until the resurrection of the First World War. Building on the West Coast had ended four years before.

The demise of the small sailing vessel was a much more complicated affair. Generally speaking, for reasons of draught, bigger crew requirements, initial capital investment, overheads and maintenance, very small steamers could not be built which could compete commercially with small wooden sailing vessels, and so the latter continued to be built and operated as long as there were small cargoes to be loaded and discharged. Because of the general scale and pattern of industry and difficulties of land transport, this situation persisted in many areas until the First World War. So in 1890 when the total of United Kingdom registered shipping came to about 8 million tons, 3 million sail and 5 million steam, about $7\frac{1}{2}$ per cent of the sailing vessel tonnage comprised wooden schooners and ketches. Between 1891 and 1913, 33 three-masted schooners were built at Porthmadog in Gwynedd for the salt fish trade from Newfoundland and in terms of quality and performance these were perhaps the finest schooners ever built in Britain. The last three-masters, the *P T Harris* and *Gestiana* were launched at Appledore and Porthmadog, respectively, as late as 1913.

These small wooden sailing vessels continued to be built in decreasing numbers in all European shipping countries until the First World War. The second of the last two types of merchant sailing ship ever to be developed – the first was the Canadian 'round stemmed tern' – appears to have been a product of the 1890s on the south west coast of Finland. This was the 'slättoppare' as she was called in Swedish, the schooner with three or more masts of approximately the same height carrying not more than one yard on her foremast. It seems most likely that the slättoppare was an independent development from the characteristic two-masted schooner, locally known as a 'galeas', of the Finnish and Swedish archipelagos and of the Åland Islands. Indeed, early vessels of this type were often registered as three-masted galeaser. Vessels with this rig were launched in Finland in the early 1890s and in 1903 the type was taken up in Denmark where it became much favoured.

British sail tonnage, still over two million tons in 1900, was down to just over one million tons by 1910 with ten and a half million tons of steam vessels. All European sailing fleets had similarly decreased, some more dramatically. The rate of abandonment of sail in Scandinavia is suggested by the statistics for the port of Stavanger. In 1880, 668 merchant sailing vessels were registered there. In 1900 there were 100, in 1914, 20. In 1870, 85 per cent of Swedish shipping was sail propelled: in 1900, 45 per cent, in 1910, 20 per cent. Only France was different. Here, 212 big steel square-rigged vessels were built or bought between 1897 and 1902 to take advantage of a government subsidy system so that they were not, strictly, commercial vessels. The merchant sailing vessel of all kinds, sizes and nationalities, was now clearly mortally sick, it seemed, and would very soon be gone.

But things are not always as they seem.

# Resurrection and the long goodbye, 1915-1965

For some months after the outbreak of the First World War in August 1914 the world freight market was paralysed while industry and ship owners waited to see what the initial effect of hostilities would be. Not until the late autumn did prospects improve, panic abate and freights begin slowly to rise. By early 1915 they were going up very satisfactorily from the shipowners' point of view. In 1914 a sailing vessel bringing lumber to western Europe from Canada took 42s 6d (£2.12½p – at 1979 prices approximately £42.50p) per standard. In late 1915 the rate was 146s (£7.30p). A year later it was 350s (£17.50p). In early 1917 pitch pine was being carried in sailing vessels from Pensacola in the Gulf of Florida to Liverpool at 476s (£23.80p) per standard, when the 1914 rate had been around 100s (£5.00). And these high freights were prepaid, that is, instead of having to borrow money to outfit for the voyage and pay interest on it, shipowners suddenly found shippers competing to pay them in advance, so that they did not only not have to pay interest, but could invest the surplus money at once in additional tonnage and earn yet more big prepaid freights.

The world's old, decrepit and uneconomical sailing vessels suddenly began to pay handsome dividends. Fortunes could be made with them. In 1916 for example, one 33-year-old 800 ton barque with a dead weight capacity of 1500 tons earned 550 per cent of her 1913 market price. In that year tonnage prices began to reflect the world freight markets and old sailing ships laid up or tottering on in a few marginal trades towards loss or dismantling suddenly became extremely valuable assets. For instance, a completely worn out 430 net ton wooden barque built by farmers on a Finnish island in 1881 which had already made her building cost many times over was sold for £300 in March 1914. Caught by the outbreak of war in Rochester she was sold in May 1916 for £1600 in laid-up state and immediately fixed to load timber in Canada for Britain at 370s a standard, which gave her a freight for the one passage of between £4000 and £5000, at least 15 times her 1914 value. In 1916 a 10-year-old 300-ton wooden three-masted schooner in bad need of a major refit which would have fetched £2000 at the most in 1914 was sold for over £18000. An 800-ton four-masted schooner was bought in the United States in 1901 for $18000 and, after earning clear profits of $44000 in sixteen years, she was sold in January 1917 for $38000. By 1919 Canadian tern schooners were getting freights of 60 dollars a ton to cross the Atlantic. In 1911 the British-built four-masted barque *Lawhill* (Plate 34) of 1892 changed hands for £5500, about £2.00 per ton gross. In 1917 she was sold for £90000, about £32.00 per ton gross, roughly four times her building cost 25 years before – the whole of her natural working life.

No wonder decaying sailing vessels of all sizes were sought out from every backwater all over the world and fitted out for sea again. But more than that, a large building programme was initiated on both sides of the Atlantic and it lasted until well after the end of the war. It was now that the schooner, after four centuries of development, in the form of the moderately sized four-master equipped with a diesel donkey engine probably the most efficient

Plate 34 (below) The steel four-masted barque *Lawhill* was one of the most successful vessels built in the last sailing ship building boom in Britain in the 1890s. Launched at Dundee in 1892 and sold to Åland owners in 1914 she fell to pieces at Lourenço Marques after the Second World War.
Photo: National Maritime Museum

Plate 35 (right) Two products of the resurrection of the merchant sailing vessel during and after the First World War. The vessel rigged ready for launching is the four-masted schooner *Francis L Taussig* and the vessel in frame is the four-master *Bradford E Jones* and they were photographed under construction at Boothbay Harbour, Maine, in 1918.
Photo: W. J. Lewis Parker

Plate 36 The five-masted schooner *Mary H Diebold*, seen coming up to anchor in Hampton Roads, Virginia, was also a product of the wartime resurrection of the sailing vessel. She was built at Newcastle, Maine, in 1920.
Photo: National Maritime Museum

Plate 37 A European product of the resurrection of the sailing vessel was the 'Skonertskepp' *Svea* built at Finström in the Åland Islands in 1920. She is here shown on a breezy day deep laden with a big deck cargo of timber.
Photo: Ålands Sjöfartsmuseum

merchant sailing ship which has ever existed, really came into her own; of the hundreds of new sailing vessels built, all were schooners, save for two steel four-masted barques, four barques, one full-rigged ship and 30 or 40 or so barquentines. The great majority were wooden, for this was a resurrection not only of the sailing vessel, but also of wooden shipbuilding and it took place largely in countries where suitable timber was still available and where sufficient elderly survivors of the ancient crafts could be assembled to teach and supervise men not skilled in the necessary trades. Great Britain played no part in this resurrection of sail. The new tonnage rapidly constructed in the United Kingdom was driven by triple expansion steam engines.

The scale of sailing ship building between 1916 and 1921 was vast and it is best expressed in bald figures. On the west coast of North America, 99 very big five-masters, 56 four-masters, three six-

masters, eight big three-masters and 16 four- and five-masted barquentines were launched. In the eastern United States, 133 four-masters were launched (Plate 35), ten five-masters (Plate 36), many big three-masters and a dozen or more very big barquentines. In eastern Canada, 323 schooners were built, the great majority of them terns, but with a dozen or more four-masters amongst them and at least two barquentines. In Denmark 12 wooden four-masted schooners, some big steel schooners and an unknown number of smaller vessels were built while a wooden full-rigged ship and a four-masted wooden schooner were built in Thailand for Danish owners. In Germany, after the war's end a number of steel three-, four- and five-masted schooners and a steel four-masted barque were built. Another four-masted barque had been launched in 1917. In Finland, at least 24 three- and four-masted schooners (Plate 37) were built besides four barques. In Holland big steel four-masted schooners were still being launched in the mid-1920s. In Greece, Italy and Spain considerable numbers of schooners, barquentines and ketches were built. So between 1916 and the early '20s at least 800 big sailing vessels and an unknown number of smaller ones were launched. The seas were full of sailing ships again and to some people in such places as the small ports of Nova Scotia and Denmark it seemed as if the great days had come back.

Those who built soon enough made enormous gains. To quote one example, a four-masted schooner was built at Thomaston, Maine, in 1917, for a contract price of $110 000. Before she was finished, she was sold for $150 000. Her first voyage, to South Africa with a general cargo, earned her a prepaid freight of $225 000. This story could be repeated many times. But after the war, the world's shipyards met the world demand for tonnage, steam and motor, much more quickly than many shipowners and investors had thought remotely possible and many of those whose vessels were delivered after 1919 were very badly caught out. As some fortunes had been made, so other fortunes were lost as sail tonnage rapidly depreciated in value in the face of collapsing freight markets. The new world fleet of big sailing vessels withered away almost as quickly as it had blossomed forth.

The few remaining big British steel square-rigged vessels, survivors of the First World War and the years immediately preceding it, did not long survive the post-war depression, and the last to be registered at a home port in the United Kingdom, the full-rigged ship *William Mitchell*, was broken up in 1927. Some steam auxiliary wooden barques and barquentines, relics of an earlier age, survived in operation in the Newfoundland seal fishery until the Second World War, as did one or two similar vessels in the Greenland trade from Denmark. The subsidised French square-rigged sailing vessels ceased operation

Plate 38 The main deck of the four-masted schooner *Helen Barnet Gring*, built at Camden, Maine, in 1919, at sea. She survived as a working vessel until she was wrecked off Cuba in 1940. Note the open rail on carved stanchions characteristic of many of the big United States schooners. A very fine model of this vessel is on display in the National Maritime Museum. Photo: Francis E. Bowker

with the First World War. One German company kept steel four-masted barques in trade to the west coast of South America until the 1930s, but a degree of concealed subsidy is probably revealed by the fact that when the *Padua*, the last steel four-masted barque ever to be built for commercial purposes, was launched in 1926 she cost considerably more to build than a steam vessel of comparable cargo capacity.

But there were some survivors of the economic blizzard, and, because of the great war-time and post-

war building boom, the big merchant sailing vessel did not vanish in the second decade of this century, as had seemed inevitable, but lingered on into the fifth. After the collapse of the post-war boom a substantial number of three-, four- and five-masted schooners remained in commission under the United States and Canadian flags (Plate 38). They did well out of the brief Miami boom of the mid-1920s. But slowly the fleet dwindled, with increasing rapidity during the years of the Great Depression, so that by 1941 only a few were left. The last of these big schooners to earn a living at sea was the *Frederick P Elkin*, a three-master built in Nova Scotia and last owned in Barbados. She made her last passage with cargo, coal from Newport News to Barbados in 1947. These schooners comprised one of the two last fleets of large merchant sailing vessels in the western world.

The other fleet was in Europe. Here, in the extra-ordinary economic and social circumstances of the Åland Islands in the Finnish Archipelago in the mouth of the Gulf of Bothnia, the big merchant sailing vessel, steel barques, wooden barques and wooden schooners both big and small, survived in numbers until the 1930s in the contemporaneously famous Australian grain and Baltic timber fleets (Plate 39) which included well-known British and German vessels of the generation before the First World War like the four-masted barques *Lawhill* and *Pommern*. Here, a merchant shipping industry began to develop only with the release from trading restrictions after the Crimean War. Capital generation was necessarily slow, and it was not until 1927 that one of the leading local shipowning families began continuous investment in steam tonnage. The names of Gustaf Erikson of Mariehamn and Hugo and Arthur Lundquist of Mariehamn and Vårdö go down to history as the last great owners of big sailing vessels in Europe. The descendants of the sailing ship men in Åland today own a very efficient modern fleet which comprises about a third of the merchant shipping tonnage of Finland, though the last sailing voyages were made, very unprofitably, as late as 1949 with the four-masted barques *Pamir* and *Passat*. Today the British-built steel four-masted barque *Pommern* lies in Mariehamn alongside the Ålands Sjöfartsmuseum just as she came in from the sea in 1939, the only unchanged big steel square-rigged merchant sailing ship in the world and the finest preserved merchant ship. There is an excellent model of her, made in Åland, in the National Maritime Museum.

In only one other area did big sailing vessels of European and American type remain commercially profitable in significant numbers until the end of the 1930s. A fleet of wooden barques, brigs, brigantines and full-rigged ships of from about 200 to 700 tons

Plate 39 The barque *Sverre* of Vårdö, Åland, built at Nystad in 1872, was the last barque and the last composite-built vessel to carry cargo at sea. She was lost on the Baltic skerries off Lågskär on 7 December 1941.
Photo: National Maritime Museum

net operated on the east coast of India and in the Bay of Bengal through the early years of this century and a few of them survived into its second half. They worked on the coast of Ceylon, to Malabar, to Thailand, Tuticorin, and to the coast of Madras. Their big annual cargo was a yearly rice lift from Burma to Ceylon and India. It is impossible to determine their numbers, but probably several score of them were sailing in the 1920s and early '30s. It was appropriate that they should be one of the last groups of square-rigged merchant ships, for down to the end they carried single topsails, studdingsails and skysails – the rig of the new ships of the 1850s, which they also resembled in hull form. They had natural fibre standing rigging without ratlines on the shrouds (Plate 40). They navigated, like the *Civility*, page 10, by sailing down the latitude. Many of them were built in and soon after the resurrection boom of the First World War. In 1937 a barquentine was built with single topsail on the fore and a jibboom a third as long as the vessel, and there may have been others built even later. Like the Baltic sailing timber ships of the same period, freights were high enough to give them a good enough living with two or three passages a year. The world's last traditional square-rigged merchant ship to earn her living from freights was one of these vessels – a beautiful brigantine which in every respect resembled a British vessel of the 1840s and which was still sailing without an engine in the mid-1950s. When I saw her sail into Colombo Harbour in 1952 in appearance at least she was a worthy last survivor of all the square-rigged merchant vessels in history.

It was the small sailing vessel which really said the long goodbye. No small powered vessel could be built to profit from the centuries old trade with salt cod across the North Atlantic from Newfoundland to Europe. In the last century over the years hundreds of British schooners had sailed in this trade, and in the 20th century wooden schooners continued to be built in Welsh and Devon yards and many Dutch steel three-masters were launched for this particular business. But after the 1914–18 war the trade became the preserve of Nova Scotian and Danish schooners, built during the war time boom or just after it. In the middle of 1928 there were over 40 of these ships on their way across the Atlantic together. It was not until the end of the Second World War that the work of small schooners on the North Atlantic came to an end and indeed occasional fixtures of Danish wooden schooners with salt fish cargoes from Labrador to Europe were still being made in 1950.

In short sea trades vessels using sails were to persist even longer. The reason was a development not foreseen in 1914. By then there were already a number of small vessels which had been equipped with

auxiliary oil motors of various kinds, mostly semi-diesels of the hot bulb variety. Again, an example of this type of motor is on display in the National Maritime Museum. After the war this new form of marine propulsion became widespread and it prolonged the life of the small merchant sailing ship until the middle of the century, and even after, and led, particularly in Holland, Denmark and Sweden, to the building of a relatively larger number of new vessels.

The effect of the auxiliary engine was complex, but where the investment in an old vessel was low, or where there were cargoes to be carried between islands or on coasts with particularly bad land communications, or where manning legislation, etc., particularly favoured the vessel equipped with sails, as in Sweden, the auxiliary schooner and ketch with a very hardworking master who was a shareholder and had no shore overheads to carry remained profitable, even in the 1920s and 30s, even to a degree which made the construction of new tonnage commercially worthwhile. As these conditions ceased to apply, through the wearing out of old vessels, the improvement of land communications, the deaths of the men to whom this was a way of life, and the changing of laws, so the schooners and ketches dropped out of use.

The last British square-rigged merchant ship to operate commercially, the wooden barquentine *Waterwitch* of Fowey in Cornwall, owned by Edward Stephens of that port—again there is a model in the National Maritime Museum—(Plate 41) made her last passage with cargo in 1936, but at the outbreak of the Second World War there were still 100 schooners and ketches fitted with auxiliary motors, some trading smacks which operated almost like 18th-century coasters, and three sailing schooners without motors trading on the coasts of Britain. By 1960 the last of them had ceased to carry cargoes at

Plate 40 This brig, the name of which is not known, was typical of the large fleet of square-rigged vessels still trading in the Indian ocean in the 1930s and even after the Second World War.
Photo: National Maritime Museum

Plate 41 (below) The *Waterwitch* was built as a collier brig at Poole, Dorset, in 1871. Converted to the handier and more economical barquentine-rig in 1884 she survived to become the last working square-rigged merchant sailing ship to be registered at a home port in the United Kingdom.
Photo: National Maritime Museum

Plate 42 The ketch *Shamrock*, built at Plymouth in 1899 and rebuilt at Cotehele within the Port of Plymouth in 1979 by the National Trust and the National Maritime Museum and owned jointly by them, lying in her berth at Cotehele in 197
Photo: Basil Greenhill

Plate 43 The French schooner *La Mouette* of Tréguier, with her roller reefing square topsail, clearly visible in the photograph, was typical of the fleet of schooners from Brittany which continued to trade to Wales until the Second World War. Photo: H.Oliver Hill

Plate 44 The galease (ketch) *Havet* was typical of the last generation of Danish sailing vessels in rig and general form and was considered the finest of them. She was built at Svendborg in 1939 for the Danish coastal trade. Photo: Basil Greenhill collection

sea. Today one or two are preserved as memorials to the vanished age of the sailing ship. The best of these is the little ketch *Shamrock* (Plate 42).

In the 20th century in the local trade of the St Lawrence in Quebec, the auxiliary 'goelette à fond plat', a kind of reincarnation of the medieval cog, but schooner rigged, was developed as a uniquely Canadian contribution to the later history of the sailing ship. On the coasts of Italy and Spain, among the Greek Islands and on the coasts of the Levant, in the West Indies and on the coast of Newfoundland, auxiliary sailing vessels, and even a few without engines, were still to be found into the 1950s. A fleet of ketches and of schooners equipped with roller reefing square topsails continued to carry pit props and onions from ports in Brittany to South Wales until the Second World War (Plate 48). A few London River sprit-rigged sailing barges traded until

the late 1960s. Although not strictly merchant ships, big wooden barquentines fished the Newfoundland Banks from St Malo until 1939. Portuguese three and and four-masted schooners persisted in the same business into the 1970s.

Wooden three-masted schooners and ketches (Plate 44) continued to be built in Denmark until the end of the 1940s. In 1950 there were still nearly 600 Danish schooners and ketches in commission, some of them in trans-Atlantic trade. Not until the early 1960s did this great fleet finally succumb to the rising costs of labour and of sails and rigging, the building of bridges between the Danish Islands, the establishment of scheduled roll-on roll-off ferries, and changing practices in packaging, marketing and distribution. It had been left to the Danes to conduct the final obsequies of the merchant sailing ship in the western world.

# Epilogue

After some 3000 years the merchant sailing vessel, as recorded in the volumes in this series, had come to an end. All that is left is a few preserved vessels, a few hulks (Plate 45) and the fading memories of the survivors of a race of men, and women, whose occupations and way of life set them even more apart from their fellow human beings than the seafarer is set today. The skills of these people may now seem incredible, as do their attitudes of mind. For generation after generation they were despised by their contemporaries ashore. Theirs was an almost medieval way of life, fearfully arduous, dangerous and often squalid by late 20th-century standards. Indeed these men and women might be regarded as an eccentric breed, alienated from the bulk of the human race on land, for 'the sea is where you are pushed'.

None the less, they will be forever associated with a splendid instrument of man's making – sometimes powerfully beautiful, almost never ugly – the commercial sailing vessel, in all its aspects, now a cherished part of the mythology of the modern world.

Edmund Eglinton spent 15 years in wooden sailing vessels, and then in 1930 came ashore to become a successful building contractor. Reminiscing nearly 50 years later about his first job in the smack-rigged River Severn sailing barge – known locally as a trow – *Providence*, built at Tewkesbury, Gloucester, in 1829, he wrote:

Here was one of the scores of vessels that every week could be seen sailing up and down past our coast, but the first I had ever been aboard. The wonder of it all! Everything seemed so huge, so heavy, and so mighty; my arms would not encircle the mast. Then the mass of rope, big and small and chain and wire. The canvas of the sails, the like of which I had observed so many times shaking in the wind as the vessels off our shore went about and appeared to be like silken curtains trembling in a breeze, proved to be so thick and tough that I could not even bend a single fold with my puny little hands. . . . My father took me down to his cabin. I vividly remember the gleaming brass lamp with a tall glass chimney which swung on gimbals supported by a bracket from the side panelling.

Then there was the shelf with the shining brass rail that swept in a lovely curve round the after end of the cabin. Also a small black range on which stood the steaming kettle. The deckhand came down and made some tea by the simple method of throwing a handful of tea direct into the boiling water of the kettle. Then the mate came down and the four of us had tea and biscuits together, tea which came straight from the kettle and biscuits which had to be soaked.

Then the smell! Everywhere I went, on deck or below, it was there, not an objectionable odour, yet one that took some getting used to. I knew afterwards that the smell was a combination of odours from stockholm tar, oakum, pitch and all kinds of rope and twine containing tar and maybe creosote. Not only did it pervade the whole ship but one's clothes were soon impregnated.

That day I caught that incurable malady, the love of ships and sails and the smell of oakum. I have it still after nigh on seventy years.

Plate 45 In the late 20th century the hulls of old sailing vessels can still be found serving various purposes, or derelict and abandoned, in remote backwaters of the world. In 1979 the wooden barque *Kristina*, built at Göteborg in 1874 for the coffee trade from Brazil, lies slowly rotting away in Östervik, Grunsunda, on the Island of Vårdö in Åland. Note the square bow port through which timber cargoes were loaded. This was closed and the seams around it caulked before the vessel put to sea. Photo: Basil Greenhill

# Index

*Page references in italics refer to illustrations*

*Aberdeen*, 3, *39*, *40*
*Acacia*, *36*
*Afon Alaw*, *41*
*Afon Cefni*, *41*
*A G Ropes*, *34*
*A J Fuller*, *36*
*Alden Besse*, *23*
American Civil War, 23, 33, 34, 35, 37
*Archibald McMillan*, *25*, 26
*Archibald Russell*, *44*, 45
*Ariel*, 32
*Asta*, *29*
auxiliary semi-diesels, 55
Bale, Richard, 10
Barry, *44*
Bath, Me., *23*, *38*
*Beethoven*, 45
*Bertha L Downs*, *38*
*Bessemer*, *41*
Boer War, 45
*Bradford E Jones*, *50*
Bristol, *11*, 14, 16, 17, 18, 29, 40
*British Shipping*, 32
*Charles W Morgan*, 19
*Civility*, 10, 37, 54
*Clara*, *14*
*Colleen*, *36*
Companies Act, 22
Conrad, Joseph, 45
*Cotehele*, *56*
*Countess of Bective*, 6
*Crescent*, *36*
Crimean War, 22, 23, 24, 53
*Cutty Sark*, 32
donkey engine, diesel, 49
donkey engine, steam, 28, *39*, *44*, 46

*Donola*, 32
*Driver*, 17
Eglinton, Edmund, 58
electric telegraph, 24
Ellis, William, 13, 14
*Emma*, *21*
Erikson, Gustaf, 53
*E R Sterling*, 47
*Favell*, *40*
*Francis L Taussig*, *50*
*Frau Minna Petersen*, *35*
*Frederick P Elkin*, 53
*Gestiana*, 48
goelette, 57
*Grace Harwar*, *40*
*Great Britain*, 18, 30
*Havet*, *54*
*Helen Barnet Gring*, *52*
Holt, Alfred, 32
*Humility*, *36*
*Inca*, *39*
Indian ocean brig, *55*
*Jane Banks*, *34*
*Jesse Murdock*, *23*
*John Pritchard*, 37
*Kristina*, *59*
*La Mouette*, 57
*Lawhill*, 49, *50*, 53
Levick, Edwin, 26
*Liberty*, 6, 7
*Lizzie Trenberth*, *25*, 26
*Looe*, 16
Lundquist, Hugo and Arthur, 53
*Margaret Jones*, *44*
*Mary*, 6, 7
*Mary Ann Peters*, *11*, 12
*Mary Dugdale*, 6
*Mary E Lynch*, 37

*Mary H Diebold*, *51*
*Maryport*, *29*
*Massachusetts*, 9
Merchant Shipping Acts, 10, 12, 14, 18, 20, 24
*Mitchelgrove*, *21*
*Montrosa*, *31*
*Moshulu*, 45
*Mozart*, 45, *46*
Napier's yard, 3
Napoleonic Wars, 12, 14, 19
Navigation Act, 22
New Bedford Harbour, *9*
*Nigger of the Narcissus, The*, 45
*Ocean Queen*, *36*
Pacific Steam Navigation Co., 32
*Padua*, 52
*Pamir*, 53
*Passat*, 53
'Patent' windlass, 28
*Pommern*, 53
*Providence*, 58
Porth Gaverne, *15*
*Portishead*, *29*
*P T Harris*, 48
*Reliant*, 32
*Rendova*, 45
roller reefing, 37, *57*
*Sela*, 26
*Serica*, 32
*Shamrock*, *56*, 57
Siemens, *41*
*Sigyn*, *33*
*Sir Lancelot*, 32
slättoppare, 48
'Sound dues', 24
South West India Dock, *42–43*

Spanish–American War, 47
Stephens & Son, Alex., *41*
Stephens, Edward, 55
Stephens, John, 4
Suez Canal, 3, 33, 34
*Sunlight*, 45
*Superb*, 13, 14, 16, 19, 26
*Svea*, *51*
*Sverre*, *54*
Swansea, 6, 7, 8, 14, 18
*Taeping*, 32
*Telegraph*, 15
'tern schooner', *39*, 48, 49, 51
*Thermopylae*, 32
Thornton, R.H., 32
*Times*, 36
triple expansion engines, 5, *39*, *40*, *44*, *51*
*Victoria*, *16*, 26
Villiers, Alan, 46
Virginia railway, 48
War of 1812, 19

# THE SHIP

The first seven titles in this major series of ten books on the development of the ship are: 2. *Long Ships and Round Ships: Warfare and Trade in the Mediterranean, 3000 BC–500 AD*, by John Morrison; 4. *The Century before Steam: The Development of the Sailing Ship 1700–1820*, by Alan McGowan; 5. *Steam Tramps and Cargo Liners: 1850–1950*, by Robin Craig; 6. *Channel Packets and Ocean Liners: 1850–1970*, by John Maber; 7. *The Life and Death of the Merchant Sailing Ship: 1815–1965*, by Basil Greenhill; 8. *Steam, Steel and Torpedoes: the Warship in the 19th Century*, by David Lyon; and 9. *Dreadnought to Nuclear Submarine*, by Antony Preston.

The remaining three books, which are to be published in 1981, will cover: 1. Ships in the ancient world outside the Mediterranean and in the medieval world in Europe (to the 15th century), by Sean McGrail; 3. The ship, from *c*.1420–*c*.1700, by Alan McGowan; and 10. The Revolution in Merchant Shipping, 1950–1980, by Ewan Corlett.

All titles in *The Ship* series are available from:

HER MAJESTY'S STATIONERY OFFICE
*Government Bookshops*
49 High Holborn, London WC1V 6HB
13a Castle Street, Edinburgh EH2 3AR
41 The Hayes, Cardiff CF1 1JW
Brazennose Street, Manchester M60 8AS
Southey House, Wine Street, Bristol BS1 2BQ
258 Broad Street, Birmingham B1 2HE
80 Chichester Street, Belfast BT1 4JY

*Government publications are also available through booksellers*

The full range of Museum publications is displayed and sold at
National Maritime Museum
Greenwich

Obtainable in the United States of America from Pendragon House Inc.
2595 East Bayshore Road
Palo Alto
California 94303

HMSO BOOKS

Two masted schooner
with single topsail and
flying topgallant

Three masted schooner with double
topsails and standing topgallant

Six masted schooner

# Fore and Aft rig

late 19th century

Feet   150   125   100   75   50   25   0   25

Metres   60   50   40   30   20   10   0   10